T0146304

Olympic-Caliber Cybersecurity

Lessons for Safeguarding the 2020 Games and Other Major Events

Cynthia Dion-Schwarz, Nathan Ryan, Julia A. Thompson, Erik Silfversten, Giacomo Persi Paoli

For more information on this publication, visit www.rand.org/t/RR2395

Library of Congress Cataloging-in-Publication Data is available for this publication.
ISBN: 978-1-9774-0165-6

Published by the RAND Corporation, Santa Monica, Calif.
© Copyright 2018 RAND Corporation
RAND® is a registered trademark.

Cover: resnow, kras99 / Adobe Stock.

Support RAND
Make a tax-deductible charitable contribution at
www.rand.org/giving/contribute

www.rand.org

Preface

This report profiles the cybersecurity threat landscape faced by Japan as the host nation of the 2020 Summer Games and 2020 Paralympic Games of the XXXII Olympiad. The overarching objective of the study was to produce a threat actor typology, based on a risk assessment of the Tokyo 2020 threat landscape. Synthesizing multiple sources of primary and secondary data, the study team developed a visualization of the threat landscape that provides an at-a-glance overview to guide Olympic security planners, computer emergency response teams, and policy- and decisionmakers as they prioritize and address cybersecurity threats. The risk assessment also considered the motivation, sophistication, and propensity of threat actors to collude with one another.

This research could be valuable to a wide variety of stakeholders and will be of particular interest to stakeholders involved in planning and ensuring the security of the Tokyo 2020 Games. The research also serves as a reference to inform ongoing policy debates on cybersecurity preparations for mega-events and as a basis for future research.

RAND Ventures

RAND is a research organization that develops solutions to public policy challenges to help make communities throughout the world safer and more secure, healthier and more prosperous. RAND is non-profit, nonpartisan, and committed to the public interest.

RAND Ventures is a vehicle for investing in policy solutions. Philanthropic contributions support our ability to take the long view, tackle tough and often-controversial topics, and share our findings in innovative and compelling ways. RAND's research findings and recommendations are based on data and evidence, and therefore do not necessarily reflect the policy preferences or interests of its clients, donors, or supporters.

Funding for this venture was provided by the generous contributions of the RAND Center for Asia Pacific Policy (CAPP) Advisory Board, and conducted within CAPP, part of International Programs at the RAND Corporation.

Support for this project was also provided, in part, by the income earned on client-funded research and other donors.

Contents

Figures, Tables, and Boxes

Figures

Tables

Boxes

Summary

This report profiles the cybersecurity threat landscape of the Tokyo 2020 Summer Games and Paralympic Games of the XXXII Olympiad. The overarching objective of the study was to produce a set of policy options tailored to the different contexts under which cyber threats to Tokyo 2020 could occur, as well as likely types of threats and threat actors. As part of our analysis, we produced a threat actor typology—a classification of actors with the potential to threaten the security of the games—based on a risk assessment of the Tokyo 2020 threat landscape. A key contribution of this research is a visualization of this threat actor typology in a format that communicates visually to Olympic security planners, computer emergency response teams, and policy- and decisionmakers the cybersecurity threats they may face.

The organizational structure of Japan's cybersecurity policy community brings together government, critical national infrastructure, and industry to secure cyberspace. These key stakeholders and their interrelationships are shown in Figure S.1.

Our risk assessment of the Japanese cybersecurity threat landscape identified four high-level threat categories to prioritize in the run-up to Tokyo 2020:

- **Targeted attacks**, aimed at high-profile Olympic assets, individuals, or organizations (e.g., broadcasting systems, Olympic commissioners, Japanese cybersecurity organizations), for either financial or political gain, could result in severe breaches or financial or reputational losses.

Figure S.1
Japan's Cybersecurity Policymaking Structure

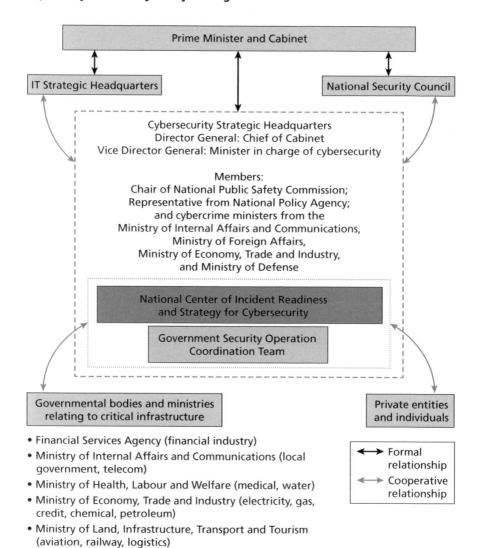

SOURCE: Adapted from Tsuyoshi Enomoto, director, Information Science and
Technology, Japanese Ministry of Education, Culture, Sports, Science and Technology,
"Cybersecurity Strategy in Japan and Countermeasures for Cyber Threats by MEXT,"
presentation slides, November 1, 2016, slide 4.

- **Distributed denial of service (DDoS) attacks** against Tokyo 2020 infrastructure or associated networks could disrupt the availability of services or distract from other ongoing attacks. DDoS attacks could be launched by advanced threat actors, such as nation-states, or less sophisticated groups, such as hacktivists.[1] Particular attention should be paid to developments in DDoS methods, including Internet of Things–powered botnets.
- **Ransomware attacks** could affect a wide range of devices, services, and underlying infrastructure supporting the Tokyo 2020 Olympics, including participant and visitor devices, transportation services, and point-of-sale systems.
- **Cyber propaganda or misinformation** could be deployed to cause reputational loss for individuals, sponsor organizations, or the host nation. It could also be deployed for political purposes or to disrupt the Olympic Games themselves.

This report also examines lessons from previous Olympic Games. As Olympic organizers' reliance on information and communications technology (ICT) infrastructure has steadily increased over successive games, so too have cybersecurity requirements. Despite a proliferation of adversary capabilities, the Olympic Games have yet to suffer a successful high-impact, high-profile cyberattack.[2] Based on the relative success of Olympic cybersecurity planners so far, we identified five general categories of lessons for Tokyo 2020:

1. Plan early so there is sufficient time to assess event-specific threats, build trust and a community of stakeholders, and establish mechanisms and processes for information sharing, incident reporting, and problem resolution.

---

[1] *Hacktivist* is a portmanteau of *hacker* and *activist*.

[2] Numerous cyberattacks have targeted Olympic infrastructure, attendees, participants, and VIPs since 2010, however. For example, a 40-minute DDoS attack on July 27, 2012, attempted but failed to take down the London Olympic Park's power systems during the games' opening ceremony. The 2016 Rio games saw cybercriminals defrauding victims, as well as data leaks from government and Olympics-related organizations; however, attackers did not directly target Olympic ICT infrastructure.

2. Prioritize cooperation and information sharing, particularly by drawing in private-sector stakeholders, recognizing that there is no single owner or stakeholder in Olympic cybersecurity.
3. Create a shared mission and common cybersecurity goal to help bolster trust and individual stakeholders' openness and commitment to information sharing.
4. Establish clear roles and responsibilities among stakeholders to help them understand how to support the common goal and respond to specific challenges.
5. Incorporate cybersecurity into broader security planning, training, and exercises right from the start.

Table S.1 presents the synthesized findings of our risk assessment and each of its constituent elements. It lists the identified threat actors, their quantified level of risk (likelihood and impact), and a risk prioritization and ranking of the threats, from most to least threatening.

We prioritized the threat actors who pose the greatest potential risk to cyber infrastructure and networks for Tokyo 2020 planners. Foreign intelligence services—should they choose to act—pose the greatest threat, with a high level of technical sophistication and the potential to have a large impact. Cyberterrorists and cybercriminals are also of concern, although less so than foreign intelligence services. Cyberterrorists have only a moderate level of technological sophistication, but their potential impact on the games could be severe. And while cybercriminals possess high levels of technical skill, we assessed both the likelihood and potential impact of these attacks as only "medium." Although they are newsworthy when they do occur, we judged attacks from hacktivists and insider threats as carrying a lower risk to the games. Finally, ticket scalpers are likely to exploit cyber vulnerabilities for profit, but their overall threat to the security of the games is low when compared with other actors. Figure S.2 visualizes the data in Table S.1, showing the sophistication, risk, and motivations of cyber threat actors with respect to the Tokyo 2020 games.

Table S.1
A Prioritized Risk Assessment of Tokyo 2020 Based on a Typology of Hackers

Threat Actor	Adversary Motivation	Risk Analysis			Risk Evaluation	
		Sophistication	Likelihood	Impact	Prioritization	Rank
Foreign intelligence services	Ideology	High	Medium	High	High	1
Cyberterrorists	Ideology/revenge	Medium	Medium	High	Medium	2
Cybercriminals/organized crime	Profit	High	Medium	Medium	Medium	3
Hacktivists	Ideology/revenge	Medium	Medium	Medium	Medium	4
Insider threats	Revenge/profit	Medium	Low	Medium	Medium	5
Ticket scalpers	Profit	Medium	High	Low	Low	6

Figure S.2
Cyber Threats to the Tokyo 2020 Games

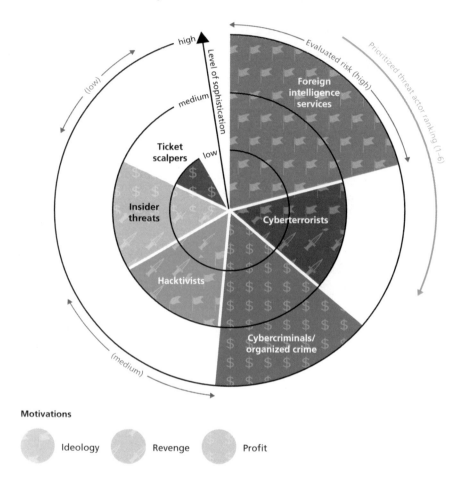

The policy options presented in this report are clustered around two themes: general policy options for Olympic cybersecurity planners and specific policy options related to Tokyo 2020. The general policy options are as follows:

1. **Plan early.** The earlier cybersecurity planning and preparation begins, the more time there is to assess event-specific threats, shape a community of stakeholders and build trust among

them, and establish mechanisms and processes for information sharing, incident reporting, and problem resolution.

2. **Cooperate and share information.** There are a number of cybersecurity stakeholders in the public and private sectors who must collaborate, cooperate, and share information to reduce cybersecurity risks in advance of the Olympic Games. Government and Olympic planners should seek to include private-sector stakeholders in any cybersecurity cooperation and information-sharing arrangements to effectively mitigate cybersecurity risks.

3. **Know the mission and have a common security goal.** For a successful public-private, multi-stakeholder cybersecurity strategy to succeed, all parties must understand and buy into a common goal. Sharing a mission can bolster trust and increase individual stakeholders' openness and commitment to information sharing.

4. **Clearly define all stakeholder roles and responsibilities, and revisit them throughout the preparation and execution of the games.** Defining clear roles and responsibilities helps stakeholders better understand how best to contribute to the broader mission and ensures that they know to whom to refer specific challenges or incidents. For example, before the Rio 2016 games, the Brazilian National Computer Emergency Response Team circulated an email identifying four key cyber teams and their responsibilities.[3]

5. **Allocate resources to mitigate cybersecurity risks.** By taking a risk-based approach to cybersecurity, we developed a prioritized list of threat actors to consider and address as part of the planning for Tokyo 2020. Effectively reducing these risks to an acceptable level will require adequate resources that are apportioned appropriately.

---

[3] See Lucimara Desiderá, "Lessons Learned from the Rio2016 Summer Olympic Games," presentation at the San José FIRST Technical Colloquium, San José, Costa Rica, September 2016b, p. 6.

6. **Deter the riskiest adversaries with a targeted cyber defense campaign.** Our assessment indicated that the riskiest threat actors facing Tokyo 2020 are foreign intelligence services (i.e., hacking groups with either implicit or explicit support from hostile foreign nation-states) and cyberterrorists (i.e., terrorist groups that use the internet to recruit and to support ICT-related terrorist attacks). Such attackers might seek to disrupt the games and embarrass the host nation. To effectively mitigate against such an event, a targeted deterrence campaign might dissuade these adversaries from attempting to attack altogether—for example, carrying out a publicly documented cybersecurity exercise to showcase defensive preparations—and convince them that the costs of executing an attack are too high, the chances of success are too low, and the prospective retaliatory costs are unbearable.

7. **Incorporate cybersecurity into broader security planning.** Planners should incorporate cybersecurity into broader security planning efforts, training, and exercises right from the start. Planners should work to build a cybersecurity community and incorporate cyber into the broader Olympic security community, as cyberattacks can have widespread physical security effects. For instance, Tokyo 2020 security planners could test their cyber capabilities at earlier events, such as the Rugby World Cup in 2019.

We formulated these policy options to align with the Japanese government's organization and policy apparatus (as outlined in Figure S.1), which should be effective in achieving the security goals of Tokyo 2020. The capability of each ministry, body, or headquarters could be further enhanced with substantial resources and by implementing the policy options outlined here.

Acknowledgments

We are grateful for the support and funding for this project provided by the RAND Center for Asia Pacific Policy. Special thanks go to Scott W. Harold for support in identifying Japanese stakeholders. We are also grateful for the time and invaluable insights of the people we interviewed for the study. Finally, we would like to thank our quality assurance reviewers, Hans Pung, Susanne Sondergaard, Rafiq Dossani, and Scott W. Harold, who gave constructive feedback on elements of the methodology and critical review of the final report.

Abbreviations

APT	advanced persistent threat
ASN	Autonomous System Number
ATM	automatic teller machine
CCIRC	Canadian Computer Incident Response Centre
CERT	computer emergency response team
CERT.br	Brazilian National Computer Emergency Response Team
CIO	chief information officer
CSIRT	computer security incident response team
CTIR Gov	Centro de Tratamento de Incidentes de Segurança de Redes [the Brazilian government's computer security and incident response team]
DDoS	distributed denial of service
DNS	Domain Name System
DoS	denial of service
DRDC	Defence Research and Development Canada
FIFA	Fédération Internationale de Football Association
HT	handling time

ICS	industrial control system
ICT	information and communication technology
IEC	International Electrotechnical Commission
IoT	Internet of Things
IP	internet protocol
ISO	International Organization for Standardization
ISP	internet service provider
IT	information technology
JPCERT/CC	Japan Computer Emergency Response Team Coordination Center
NIC.br	Brazilian Network Information Center
PII	personally identifiable information
REA	rapid evidence assessment
VoIP	voice over internet protocol
WP	work package

CHAPTER ONE

Introduction

This report profiles the cybersecurity threat landscape faced by the Tokyo 2020 Summer Games and Tokyo 2020 Paralympic Games of the XXXII Olympiad. The overarching objective of the study was to produce a set of policy options tailored to the different contexts under which cyber threats to Tokyo 2020 could occur, as well as likely types of threats and threat actors. As part of our analysis, we produced a threat actor typology—a classification of actors with the potential to threaten the security of the games—based on a risk assessment of the Tokyo 2020 threat landscape. A key contribution of this research is a visualization of this threat actor typology, which aims to visually communicate to Japanese Olympic security planners, computer emergency response teams (CERTs), and policy- and decisionmakers the cybersecurity threats they may face.

This introductory chapter contextualizes the cybersecurity threats faced by Olympic organizers and describes the high-level research approach that we used to address the six research objectives of the study.

Cybersecurity Threats Have Emerged as a Concern for Olympic Organizers

Since at least the 2004 Athens games, cybersecurity has been a concern for Olympic host nations, the International Olympic Committee, and commercial sponsors.[1] Japan's vision to become the "most advanced urban technology metropolis in the world" underpinned its bid to host the 2020 Olympics.[2] This dependence on technology signals a shift toward an unpredictable, complex, and contested environment as more essential services rely on a continuously functioning cyberspace. More than ever, security planners must consider the cybersecurity threat landscape if they are to effectively mitigate threats, apportion limited resources, and host a resilient, safe, and secure Olympic Games.

The Olympic Games are a target-rich environment, drawing athletes from more than 200 nations and worldwide media coverage.[3] This high visibility makes the games a target for those seeking to cause politically motivated harm, enrich themselves through criminality, or embarrass the host nation on the international stage. The contemporary literature on sporting mega-events and their security challenges tends to focus on perceptions of risk, fear, and terrorism in shaping the security environment.[4] Our literature review complemented these findings with an examination of lessons learned from previous Olympic Games, which are documented in Chapter Four.[5]

---

[1]   Atos, "Atos Origin Reveals IT Systems for the ATHENS 2004 Olympic Games," press release, June 7, 2004.

[2]   Eva Kassens-Noor and Tatsuya Fukushige, "Olympic Technologies: Tokyo 2020 and Beyond: The Urban Technology Metropolis," *Journal of Urban Technology*, July 1, 2016.

[3]   Since the 2000 Sydney games, 200 or more countries have competed in each subsequent Summer Olympics (Gregory Sousa, "Numbers of Participating Countries in Olympic Games Through the Years," *WorldAtlas.com*, last updated April 25, 2017.

[4]   Tracy Taylor and Kristine Toohey, "Perceptions of Terrorism Threats at the 2004 Olympic Games: Implications for Sport Events," *Journal of Sport and Tourism*, Vol. 12, No. 2, 2007; Kristine Toohey and Tracy Taylor, "Mega Events, Fear, and Risk: Terrorism at the Olympic Games," *Journal of Sport Management*, Vol. 22, No. 4, July 2008.

[5]   More accurately, lessons have been *identified* from past Olympic Games rather than *learned*.

This Study Analyzed the Tokyo 2020 Cybersecurity Threat Landscape

The purpose of the study was to characterize the cyber threats faced by the Tokyo 2020 Olympics and to produce a threat actor typology to clearly communicate those risks to policy- and decisionmakers in Japan. The study was designed around six research objectives:

1. Analyze the cybersecurity threat landscape for the Tokyo 2020 Olympics.
2. Perform case-study reviews of cyber events at the London 2012 and Rio 2016 Olympics, as well as the Vancouver 2010 Winter Olympics.
3. Inform public policy debate in Japan to strengthen cybersecurity preparedness for the Tokyo 2020 Olympics.
4. Assess, categorize, and collate cybersecurity threat actors likely to disrupt the Tokyo 2020 games into a threat actor typology.
5. Produce an infographic visualizing the threat landscape and relevant actors.
6. Provide a basis for future research, including a risk analysis of threat actors based on their likelihood to intervene and their potential impact to inform how resources are prioritized. The study and its methods are replicable to other countries and events.

To achieve these objectives, we adopted a mixed-methods research design that blended qualitative and quantitative data collected from documentary research and interviews. (For more information on our study methods, see Appendix A.)

Structure of the Report
Figure 1.1 presents the report structure and outlines the logical link between the chapters and three appendixes.

Figure 1.1
Report Structure

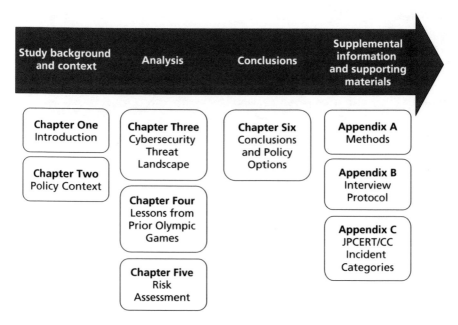

Limitations of the Analysis

Our study relied heavily on open-source data to inform the discussions of the policy context presented in Chapter Two, the Japanese cybersecurity threat landscape presented in Chapter Three, and lessons from previous Olympic Games presented in Chapter Four, as well as the projected risk assessment specific to Tokyo 2020 (Chapter Five). We conducted only a few interviews and discussions with subject-matter experts.[6] The study's findings and high-level policy options (Chapter Six) reflect a synthesis of the available open-source data. Readers should treat them as preliminary findings based on what is almost certainly only fragmentary evidence, given that we did not review classified information from any of the countries discussed in this report.

---

[6] We conducted key informational interviews with two Japanese cybersecurity subject-matter experts. We also spoke informally with several Japanese cybersecurity experts over the course of the project.

In addition, we did not have access to independent, empirical research classifying hackers into constituent subcategories. Instead, we used the literature review to examine previously published typologies and incorporated their relevant constituent parts into our study. Moreover, our use of Japan Computer Emergency Response Team Coordination Center (JPCERT/CC) data sets limited our ability to attribute computer security incidents to specific classes of threat actors, and this posed a challenge when we incorporated the data set into the risk assessment in Chapter Five.

Finally, we discuss a number of policy options in Chapter Six. These are treated as *options* rather than *recommendations,* per se, because they are intended to be suggestive, not definitive, and rely on the open-source evidence to which we had access.

CHAPTER TWO

Policy Context

"Know Thyself": The Organizational Structure and Stakeholders Involved in Securing Japan's Cyberspace

The organizational structure of Japan's cybersecurity policy community brings together government, critical national infrastructure, and industry to secure cyberspace. The structure of the key stakeholders and their relationships are shown in Figure 2.1.

- IT Strategic Headquarters was established by the Basic Act on the Formation of an Advanced Information and Telecommunications Network Society in November 2000.[1] The organization's aim is to promote "measures for forming an advanced information and telecommunications network society" and to adapt to the socioeconomic changes caused by information telecommunication technology (ICT).[2] The director general of the IT Strategic Headquarters is the prime minister. As of 2017, the headquarters oversaw the use of public- and private-sector data for the purposes of protecting privacy, security, and information sharing rights.[3]
- Japan's National Security Council was established on December 4, 2013, as a forum for "strategic discussions on various

---

[1] Prime Minister of Japan and His Cabinet, "IT Strategic Headquarters," webpage, undated(b).

[2] Government of Japan Cabinet Secretariat, Basic Act on the Formation of an Advanced Information and Telecommunications Network Society, November 29, 2000.

[3] Government of Japan Cabinet Secretariat, 2000.

national security issues," held on a regular basis or as requested by the prime minister.[4] At the same time that the administration of Prime Minister Shinzo Abe stood up the council, it also appointed a national security adviser, staffed a National Security Secretariat to support the National Security Council, and issued Japan's first-ever national security strategy.[5]

- The Cyber Security Strategic Headquarters was established by the 2014 Cybersecurity Basic Act, which entered into force in March 2016. The office was formerly known as the Information Security Policy Council.[6] The director general is the chief of cabinet and reports to the prime minister and liaises closely with the five constituent and permanent member ministries:[7]
  - National Public Safety Commission
  - Ministry of Internal Affairs and Communication on communication and network policy
  - Ministry of Foreign Affairs on diplomatic policy
  - Ministry of Economy, Trade and Industry on information policy
  - Ministry of Defence on national security issues
  - any other minister appointed by the prime minister or any expert appointment (including National Police Agency counter-cybercrime appointments).
- The National Center of Incident Readiness and Strategy for Cybersecurity was strengthened with the passage of the Cybersecurity Basic Act that rebranded the already established National

---

[4]   Japanese Ministry of Foreign Affairs, "Japan's Security Policy," webpage, undated.

[5]   J. Berkshire Miller, "How Will Japan's New NSC Work?" *The Diplomat*, January 29, 2014.

[6]   Melissa Hathaway, Chris Demchak, Jason Kerben, Jennifer McArdle, and Francesca Spidalieri, *Japan Cyber Readiness at a Glance*, Arlington, Va.: Potomac Institute for Policy Studies, September 2016, p. 5.

[7]   Prime Minister of Japan and His Cabinet, "Fundamental Structure of the Government of Japan," webpage, undated(a); Tsuyoshi Enomoto, director, Information Science and Technology, Japanese Ministry of Education, Culture, Sports, Science, and Technology, "Cybersecurity Strategy in Japan and Countermeasures for Cyber Threats by MEXT," presentation slides, November 1, 2016.

Information Security Centre. The act codified the center's tasks and functions, making it responsible for coordinating cybersecurity policies, monitoring government-related organizations that handle large volumes of personal data, and providing command and control functions in crises, especially those involving critical national infrastructure.[8] The National Center of Incident Readiness and Strategy for Cybersecurity also formulates Japan's cybersecurity strategy policy document.

- The Government Security Operation Coordination Team, part of the secretariat directed by the Cyber Security Strategic Headquarters, coordinates closely with government bodies and ministries responsible for critical infrastructure.[9] The team also monitors government networks for security vulnerabilities.

- JPCERT/CC, formed in 1996, was the first Japanese computer emergency response team/command center. JPCERT/CC engages in research and analysis to find better ways to prevent cyberattacks and limit damage from attacks. The organization coordinates with network service providers, security vendors, government agencies, and industry associations, as well as with other computer security incident response teams (CSIRTs) in the Asia-Pacific region and elsewhere. In addition, JPCERT/CC publishes weekly and quarterly incident response and analysis reports, along with other relevant computer security information.[10]

---

[8] Japanese National Information Security Policy Council, *The Second National Strategy on Information Security Aiming for Strong "Individual" and "Society" in IT Age*, February 3, 2009, p. 73.

[9] Shinsuke Akasaka, director, ICT Security Office, Japanese Ministry of Internal Affairs and Communications, "Japanese Government Cyber Security Strategy," presentation slides, January 21, 2015, slide 7.

[10] JPCERT/CC, "About JPCERT/CC," webpage, undated.

Figure 2.1
Japan's Cybersecurity Policymaking Structure

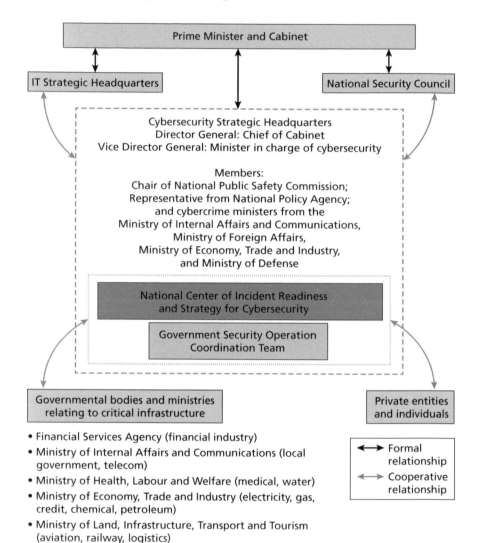

- Financial Services Agency (financial industry)
- Ministry of Internal Affairs and Communications (local government, telecom)
- Ministry of Health, Labour and Welfare (medical, water)
- Ministry of Economy, Trade and Industry (electricity, gas, credit, chemical, petroleum)
- Ministry of Land, Infrastructure, Transport and Tourism (aviation, railway, logistics)

SOURCE: Adapted from Enomoto, 2016, slide 4.

Japan's Cybersecurity Preparations for Tokyo 2020

Japan has already established measures to protect critical national infrastructure in advance of Tokyo 2020, taking steps to harden cyber defenses and protect tourists and participants. Cybersecurity plans for Tokyo 2020 have been in development since at least 2015. Plans for mitigating cybersecurity threats were first laid out in *Cybersecurity Strategy 2015*, which gave the "basic directions of Japan's cybersecurity policies for the coming three years approximately."[11] Moreover, the Ministry of Internal Affairs and Communications requested 20 billion yen (approximately $181 million) in funding for comprehensive cybersecurity measures in preparation for Tokyo 2020, highlighting the government's commitment to cybersecurity planning.[12]

Additional cybersecurity efforts in Japan include training efforts under way between the Japanese government and regional partners, including Indonesia, Laos, Myanmar, the Philippines, and Vietnam, to prepare governments to respond to cyberattacks.[13] The cybersecurity program has received three years of funding from the Japan International Cooperation Agency. Also in 2015, the Information-Technology Promotion Agency[14] estimated that 160,000 of the 265,000 information security personnel in Japan lack the skills required for their jobs. The Japanese government committed to training 50,000 people in the public and private sectors specifically to guard the country against cyberattacks during Tokyo 2020.[15]

In 2017, a new training center for cybersecurity recruits was built in Tokyo to house a hands-on cyber range, in anticipation of cyber-

---

[11] Government of Japan, *Cybersecurity Strategy 2015*, September 3, 2015.

[12] *Nikkei Asian Review*, "Japan to Deepen Ranks of Network Defenders with Eye to Olympics," July 16, 2015.

[13] Cristina Maza, "Cyber Security Training Now Underway in Japan," *Phnom Penh Post*, March 1, 2017.

[14] The Information-Technology Promotion Agency is affiliated with the Japanese Ministry of Economy, Trade and Industry. See Information-Technology Promotion Agency, "About IPA/ISEC," webpage, undated.

[15] *Nikkei Asian Review*, 2015.

attacks at the 2020 Olympics.[16] In March 2017, the Japanese government held a large-scale cybersecurity drill to simulate an actual cyber-attack involving the "world's largest" virtual network.[17] The virtual scenario included the official Tokyo 2020 website, ticket sale systems, Wi-Fi connections, and vulnerable end points (devices) in an effort to exercise Japan's defensive posture.

Even with these efforts, there has still been public concern about the government's preparedness to address a large-scale cyber incident and keep up with the evolving nature of cyber threats.[18] The new stadium, designed and built for the games, was due to be completed in November 2019—just eight months before the opening ceremony—leaving little time to conduct a full-scale exercise. These concerns have been echoed in the political domain, where there have been calls from the opposition for the government to "promptly" establish a command center for cyber countermeasures.[19]

Japan's cybersecurity planning efforts for Tokyo 2020 aim to protect critical national infrastructure, harden cyber defenses, and protect tourists and participants. These cybersecurity threat mitigation efforts are complemented by a series of policy initiatives to secure cyberspace for Tokyo 2020, outlined in the next section.

Current Policy Initiatives to Secure Cyberspace for Tokyo 2020

The government of Japan's 2015 cybersecurity strategy outlines the "basic directions of Japan's cybersecurity policies," with a vision toward

---

[16] See Sara Barker, "Japan Cybersecurity Skills Shortage in a 'State of Urgency' Before 2020 Olympics," *Security Brief Asia*, February 7, 2017, and Ian Murphy, "Japan Trains Cyber Teams for 2020 Olympics," *Enterprise Times*, February 7, 2017.

[17] *Japan Times*, "Government to Hold Massive Anti-Cyberattack Drill for 2020 Tokyo Olympics," January 5, 2017, 2017a.

[18] *Japan Times*, "Japan's Weak Cyberdefense," December 26, 2016.

[19] *Japan Times*, "With Three Years to Go, Some Worried Japan Unprepared for Olympic Cyberattack," July 21, 2017b.

securing the Tokyo 2020 Olympics.[20] The strategy is cognizant of the attention and potential increase in cybersecurity threats brought about by major international events. Its references include two Japan-hosted events: the then-upcoming 2016 Group of Seven Summit in 2016 and the 2019 Rugby World Cup. Of note, the strategy document shows a deep level of concern about the "prospect for the massive use of [Internet of Things (IoT)] systems"[21] during Tokyo 2020 and proposes sustained efforts to create secured IoT systems. It also proposes accelerating the formulation of a CSIRT for Tokyo 2020 "as a core organ responsible for making appropriate prediction and detection and for information sharing among stakeholders vital to respond appropriately against cyberattacks on relevant entities involving the management and operation" of Tokyo 2020, associated businesses, and relevant critical information infrastructure.[22]

A 2017 midterm review of the strategy refocused the policy measures that were under way by accelerating and enhancing efforts ahead of Tokyo 2020.[23] For example, the threat environment is changing and evolving in light of the proliferation of compromised IoT botnets.[24]

In responding to the changing cyber threat environment, the Cyber Security Strategic Headquarters has focused attention on the following initiatives and programs:

- A bot-cleansing campaign is aimed at comprehensively identifying affected and at-risk devices, disseminating updates and patches, and implementing an ongoing prevention campaign. Pending

---

[20] Government of Japan, 2015.

[21] Government of Japan, 2015, p. 13. The strategy defined the component parts of IoT systems as machine-to-machine devices, such as security cameras and infrastructure equipment in the energy, automotive, medical, and other relevant industries, as well as wearable devices (Government of Japan, 2015, p. 15).

[22] Government of Japan, 2015, p. 53.l

[23] National Center of Incident Readiness and Strategy for Cybersecurity, *Next Cybersecurity Strategy (Outline)*, 2017.

[24] Botnets are a network of compromised internet-connected computer devices that are used for malicious purposes, such as distributed denial of service (DDoS) attacks, stealing data, and sending spam emails.

technical and legal issues must be resolved before internet service providers (ISPs) can assist with the bot-cleansing campaign.

- A new comprehensive information-sharing and collaborative network to promote collaboration among public- and private-sector stakeholders in an effort to contain cyberattacks from metastasizing into cascading system failures. The network is predicated on information-sharing agreements, which may require changes to relevant legislation.
- An Olympic-Paralympic CSIRT will be established by March 2019 to assist the Tokyo 2020 Organising Committee on cybersecurity issues. The CSIRT will consist of specially trained staff who will collaborate with external partners, service providers, and security vendors.
- A security information center will be stood up in the National Police Agency to support evidence collection, analysis, and evaluation of physical security incidents as they arise and to liaise with other relevant organizations.

CHAPTER THREE

The Cybersecurity Threat Landscape in Japan

To further contextualize the Japanese cybersecurity landscape against the backdrop of the policy context presented in Chapter Two, this chapter provides an overview of historic and potential current cybersecurity threats. In developing this map of the threat landscape, we used a mixed-methods approach, drawing on the available literature, policy documents, case studies, and interviews. This chapter presents historical data on cyber threats and incidents in Japan to extrapolate trends that can inform the threat analysis for the Tokyo 2020 Olympics.

Introduction to the Cybersecurity Landscape

Cyberspace is an interconnected, complex, and rapidly evolving domain, and, by its very nature, it will continually morph to innovate, develop, and retain its relevance. Technological advances, including developments in artificial intelligence, the IoT, and autonomous technologies will bring additional technical, operational, strategic, and ethical challenges for mega-event organizers in the future.

Recent events have demonstrated the use of cyber capabilities in a wide range of adversary behaviors. Advanced persistent threats (APTs) and hacking campaigns targeting financial institutions and other organizations of strategic importance are proliferating and progressively difficult to detect and mitigate.

Recent hacks against sensitive Japanese targets include a 2015 attack on the Japanese pension system in which cybercriminals stole 1.25 million pension records, including such personally identifiable information (PII) as pension IDs, names, dates of birth, and even home addresses.[1] Cybercrime in Japan increased by more than 40 percent over the 12 months from March 2014 to March 2015.[2] A Trend-Micro report on cybercrime in Japan found increasing activity in dark web marketplaces, where one such site, Ken-Mou wiki@Tor, provided transactional services for child pornography, drugs, and other taboo subjects in exchange for virtual currency.[3]

Also operating within Japan's threat landscape are nation-state actors. A Mandiant report titled *APT1: Exposing One of China's Cyber Espionage Units* documents the cyberespionage campaigns, theft of trade secrets, and compromise of secure systems by an APT group backed by China's People's Liberation Army—specifically, the General Staff Department's 3rd Department (Military Cover Designator 61398).[4] APT1 has been operating internationally since 2006. The Japanese division of Symantec first publicly reported on APT1's activities, and Mandiant has since observed that APT1 has compromised 141 companies spanning 20 major industries.[5] Given APT1's active engagement in government and in the private sector, it poses a potentially significant threat to the Olympic Games.

The cybersecurity firm Cylance gave the name Operation Dust Storm to the well-organized and well-funded cyberespionage campaign targeting commercial and critical infrastructure organizations in Japan. Hackers have been targeting Japan, South Korea, and other Asian countries, as well as the United States and Europe, since 2010. According to Cylance analysts, the hackers have increased their focus on Japanese organizations in the electricity generation, oil and natural

---

[1]   Trend Micro, "Japan Pension System Gets Hacked, Exposes 1.25M Records," June 2, 2015.

[2]   Akira Urano, *The Japanese Underground*, Trend Micro, 2015.

[3]   Urano, 2015.

[4]   Mandiant, *APT1: Exposing One of China's Cyber Espionage Units*, Alexandria, Va., 2013. APT1, or PLA Unit 61398, is one of 20 APT groups identified and tracked by cybersecurity analysts worldwide.

[5]   Mandiant, 2013.

gas, transportation, finance, and construction industries since 2010.[6] At approximately the same time Mandiant released its report publicly "naming and shaming" APT1, Cylance observed a "fairly large lull" in cyberespionage activity from March 2013 to August 2013.[7] This correlation has led experts to speculate about the Chinese state's involvement in the cyberespionage Operation Dust Storm.[8]

Hacker groups can obscure the involvement of foreign state actors and their operational command of cyber campaigns. For instance, the 2016 hacks on Sony Pictures, the 2016 theft of $81 million from the Bangladesh Central Bank, and the 2017 WannaCry Ransomware attacks have shown strong links to the Lazarus Group, according to Symantec.[9] The "digital fingerprints" of the group's tools, techniques, and infrastructure point to a location in North Korea, despite Symantec claiming that the attacks "do not bear the hallmarks of a nation-state campaign but are more typical of a cybercrime campaign."[10] The *Washington Post* revealed contrary claims, stating that the U.S. National Security Agency confirmed the link between the North Korean government and the creation of the WannaCry computer worm.[11]

Even more alarming are cyberattacks that inflict physical damage on critical infrastructure. Previously regarded as just a theoretical possibility, such threats have become a reality in the form of attacks on gas

---

[6] Pierluigi Paganini, "Operation Dust Storm, Hackers Target Japanese Critical Infrastructure," *Security Affairs*, February 24, 2016.

[7] Jon Gross and Cylance SPEAR Team, *Operation Dust Storm*, Irvine, Calif.: Cylance, undated.

[8] Paganini, 2016.

[9] Symantec Security Response, "WannaCry: Ransomware Attacks Show Strong Links to Lazarus Group," *Symantec Official Blog*, May 22, 2017.

[10] Symantec Security Response, 2017. See also Nicole Perlroth, "More Evidence Points to North Korea in Ransomware Attack," *New York Times*, May 22, 2017.

[11] Ellen Nakashima, "The NSA Has Linked the WannaCry Computer Worm to North Korea," *Washington Post*, June 14, 2017.

pipelines in Turkey, a steel mill in Germany, and airports and power grids in Ukraine, among other targets.[12]

Like other developed nations, Japan faces a multifaceted and complex cybersecurity landscape. The European Network Information Security Agency Threat Taxonomy contains descriptions of more than 150 types of cyber threats, most which are also found in the Japanese threat landscape.[13]

JPCERT/CC coordinates with network service providers, security vendors, government agencies, and industry associations in Japan to gather and disseminate technical information on computer security incidents, vulnerabilities, and security fixes.

Figure 3.1 shows the number of reports, incidents, and coordinated cases in the JPCERT/CC database from 2012 to 2016. JPCERT/CC considers "Number of reports" to be the total number of reports sent through their web form, email or fax, while "Number of incidents" refers to the number of incidents in each report (multiple reports on the same incident are counted as one incident), and "Number of cases coordinated" refers to the number of cases in which coordination occurred (e.g., between JPCERT/CC and the system owner). An analysis of JPCERT/CC incident handling reports shows a number of key trends in the Japanese cybersecurity landscape and suggests key threat vectors to consider in preparing for the 2020 Tokyo Olympic Games.

Figure 3.2 presents an overview of JPCERT/CC data broken out by incident category. As shown in the figure, JPCERT/CC began recording targeted and industrial control system (ICS)–related attacks in 2015. In our risk analysis, we measure the severity of an attack type not only by its frequency but also by its potential impact. Between 2015 and 2016, JPCERT/CC recorded 188 targeted attacks on Japanese infrastructure and networks, some of which were responsible

---

[12] Evan Perez, "First on CNN: U.S. Investigators Find Proof of Cyberattack on Ukraine Power Grid," CNN, February 3, 2016; Pavel Polityuk and Alessandra Prentice, "Ukraine Says to Review Cyber Defenses After Airport Targeted from Russia," Reuters, January 18, 2016; Jordan Robertson and Michael Riley, "The Map That Shows Why a Pipeline Explosion in Turkey Matters to the U.S.," Bloomberg, December 20, 2014.

[13] European Network Information Security Agency, "Threat Taxonomy," spreadsheet, September 2016.

Figure 3.1
JPCERT/CC Overview: Number of Reports, Incidents, and Coordinated Cases
(1st quarter 2012–4th quarter 2016)

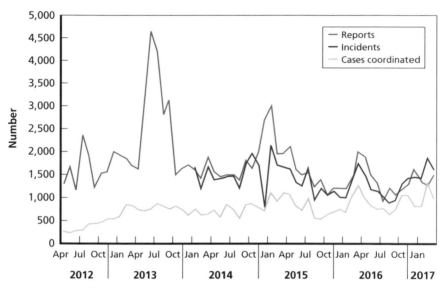

SOURCE: JPCERT/CC quarterly threat reports, 2012–2016.

for the most critical cybersecurity incidents in Japan to date. Recent prominent targeted attacks in Japan have included the Daserf APT, previously discussed Operation Dust Storm, and Operation Quantum Entanglement.[14] These attacks targeted critical Japanese industries, including power generation, oil and natural gas, construction, finance, and transportation. While the first two APT campaigns targeted more countries than Japan and had not been fully attributed at the time of this writing, technical investigative reports pointed to China as the most likely perpetrator.[15] Targeted attacks often involve spear-phishing campaigns to get access to protected networks or valuable

---

[14] Yoshihiro Ishikawa, *Cyber Grid View Technical Report: Attackers That Target Critical Infrastructure Providers in Japan*, Vol. 2, Tokyo, Japan: LAC Co., 2016; Gross and Cylance SPEAR Team, undated; Thoufique Haq, Ned Moran, Sai Vashisht, and Mike Scott, *Operation Quantum Entanglement*, Milpitas, Calif.: FireEye, 2014.

[15] Gross and Cylance SPEAR Team, undated; Ishikawa, 2016.

Figure 3.2
JPCERT/CC Incident Overview, by Incident Category (1st quarter 2012–4th quarter 2016)

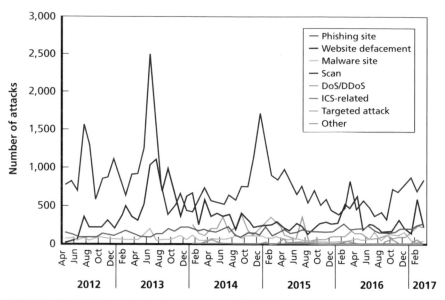

SOURCE: JPCERT/CC quarterly threat reports, 2012–2016.
NOTE: Definitions of the JPCERT/CC incident categories can be found in Appendix C.

network assets.[16] A spear-phishing campaign leading to the execution of malware on Japan Pension Service systems was the cause of one of the most severe data breaches in Japanese history, discussed earlier in this chapter.[17]

Figure 3.2 shows that the most frequent cybersecurity incidents in Japan tend to be scan activities (i.e., vulnerability searching, attempts at intrusion, and unsuccessful brute-force attacks). The high frequency of low-level threats, including scans and website defacement, in which low-risk scripts are embedded on a website, tends to distort perceptions

---

[16] *Spear phishing* refers to targeted phishing attempts in which what appear to be legitimate business emails are sent to preidentified individuals to get the targets to open a malicious attachment or link, leading to the execution of a payload.

[17] Tomoko Otake, "1.25 Million Affected by Japan Pension Service Hack," *Japan Times*, June 1, 2015.

of the threat landscape. Rarer events, such as targeted attacks and ICS-related incidents, are fewer in number but often severe and high-impact (in terms of financial damage, quantity of data stolen, political sensitivities, and disruption of service).

JPCERT/CC has also noted the persistent presence of distributed denial of service (DDoS) attacks in Japan. Registering more than 300 incidents per year, JPCERT/CC deems DDoS attacks—particularly IoT-powered DDoS attacks and Domain Name System (DNS) water-torture attacks—among the most prominent threats to Japanese cyber infrastructure.[18]

As noted, some of the most prominent APTs have been found to originate outside of Japan. JPCERT/CC data provide some insight into the geographical source of different types of attacks, as illustrated in Figure 3.3.[19] It is clear that certain attacks originate from both within and beyond Japan (e.g., phishing, malware sites) while others predominantly occur within Japan (e.g., defacing websites, scanning websites or computer networks for vulnerabilities).

The JPCERT/CC threat reports also indicate the complexity of resolving different types of incidents, highlighting perhaps not the severity of an incident but the resources required to adequately address an incident when it occurs. As illustrated in Figure 3.4, phishing site incidents were the most easily resolved, with 80 percent requiring an average handling time (HT) of 0–3 days. In contrast, both website defacements and malware site incidents required more time, with 60 percent or more requiring an average HT of 4 or more days and 30 percent of incidents requiring 11 or more days. This also does not

---

[18] Misaki Kimura, "2016 in Review: Top Cyber Security Trends in Japan," blog post, JPCERT, January 25, 2017. A DNS water torture attack is a DDoS attack method in which hijacked devices (bots) flood DNS servers with queries, preventing the server from replying to legitimate DNS queries and effectively preventing access to the targeted website.

[19] It is worth noting that these data show only where the traffic originated and not the actual attacker. It is feasible to assume that attackers could be located in a location other than the one from which the traffic originated and either routed the traffic through proxies or virtual private networks (VPNs) or used intermediaries in various geographical locations. Furthermore, the geographical origin of an attack does not necessarily indicate the nationality or motivation of an attacker.

Box 3.1
The Mirai Botnet: A Glimpse into the Future?

The IoT seeks to connect the physical and virtual worlds. Recent years have seen enormous growth in the number of internet-enabled devices and features—from smart appliances and electronics to the wireless routers that connect these devices. Poorly designed IoT devices are susceptible to malware and have been used to create large-scale botnets capable of launching vast DDoS attacks.

First detected in September 2016, Mirai malware continuously scans the internet for vulnerable IoT devices, which are then infected and used in botnet-enabled DDoS attacks. The malware uses a short list of 62 common default usernames and passwords to scan and compromise vulnerable IoT devices. Because many types of IoT devices lack proper security safeguards, the malware can compromise hundreds of thousands of devices to form a single botnet. These devices have been limited mostly to home routers and internet-enabled camera equipment, but it is feasible that these attacks could extend to any type of internet-facing device.

As the number of IoT devices continues to grow, this type of threat will only become more severe. If the current IoT trend continues, it is likely that numerous other IoT devices that use default password configurations could be easily compromised and used for botnet attacks that could severely disrupt communications or cause significant financial harm.

These types of attacks could pose two particularly challenging risks for the Tokyo 2020 Olympics:

1. IoT devices used for the Olympics could be compromised.

2. A large number of IoT devices globally could be compromised and used for DDoS attacks against devices or networks used during the Olympics.

SOURCES: US-CERT, "Security Tip (ST17-001): Securing the Internet of Things," revised November 17, 2017.

Figure 3.3
JPCERT/CC Incident Traffic Origin, by Incident Type (2015–2016)

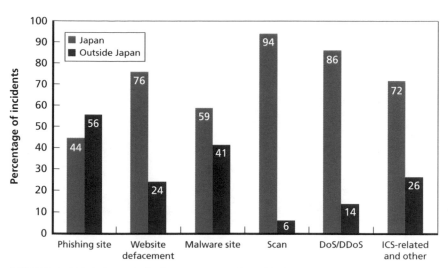

SOURCE: JPCERT/CC quarterly threat reports, 2012–2016.
NOTE: DoS = denial of service.

account for the "dwell time" (i.e., the time needed to detect an incident in the first place). Previous research has shown that dwell times can be six months or more.[20] There is little research comparing incident handling times among international CERTs, but Figure 3.4 shows a strong correlation between the increasing sophistication of a malicious incident and its subsequent handling time.

How International Experience Can Inform the Japanese Cybersecurity Threat Landscape

Cybersecurity threats are typically global phenomena, so it is imperative to consider prominent international developments when analyzing Japan's cybersecurity threat landscape. At the global level, two trends

[20] Ponemon Institute, *Advanced Threats in Retail Companies: A Study of North America and EMEA*, Traverse City, Mich., May 2015.

Figure 3.4
JPCERT/CC Average Handling Time, by Incident Type (2015–2016)

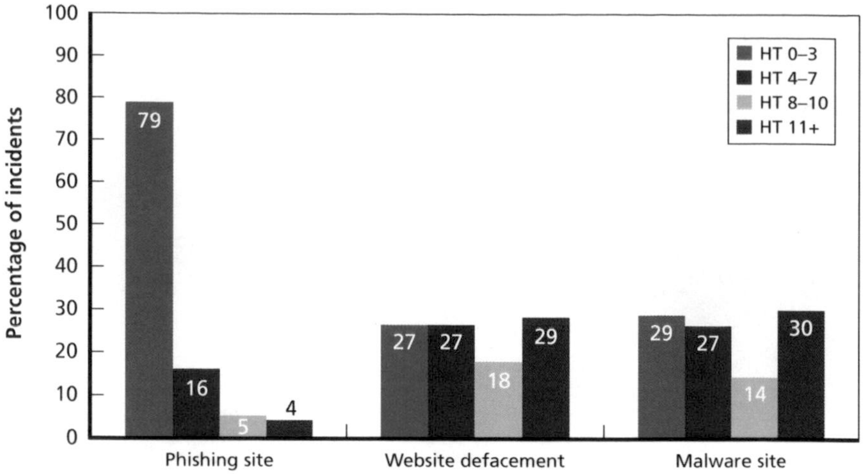

SOURCE: JPCERT/CC quarterly threat reports, 2012–2016.

stand out as particularly relevant to the Tokyo 2020 Olympics: global ransomware and cyber propaganda.

Between February and May 2017, the WannaCry ransomware resulted in tens of thousands of infections across 150 countries, including the United States, United Kingdom, Spain, Russia, Taiwan, France, and Japan.[21] When executed, the ransomware encrypts the contents of a device, rendering it unusable until a bitcoin ransom equivalent to roughly $300 is transferred to the attackers' bitcoin wallet. The WannaCry ransomware highlighted the widespread use and vulnerability of legacy devices and software and provided evidence of how quickly a threat can propagate globally.[22]

---

[21] US-CERT, "Alert (TA17-132A) Indicators Associated with WannaCry Ransomware," revised June 7, 2018. WannaCry is a threat composed of two main parts: a worm module, responsible for spreading the attack, and a ransomware module, responsible for delivering the payload. The worm module uses two types of Microsoft Windows Server Message Block (SMB) server remote code execution vulnerabilities (CVE-2017-0144 and CVE-2017-0145) to spread.

[22] Symantec, "Ransom.Wannacry," webpage, undated. Legacy or unpatched versions of Windows are still vulnerable to CVE-2017-0144 and CVE-2017-0145.

Recent events have showcased another downside of heightened connectivity and the increasing number of internet users globally: the rapid spread and dissemination of disinformation. Technology has changed the way people access, produce, and share information, an evolution reflected in debates about "fake news," "echo chambers," "computational propaganda," and similar phenomena.[23] For instance, Japan has seen the rise of an "internet far right" (*netto uyoku* or *netto hoshu*), neonationalists who voice anti-Korean views and are harshly critical of China and the mainstream media.[24] The origins of this phenomenon can be traced to backlash to the 2002 FIFA World Cup, jointly hosted by Japan and South Korea. Japan's mainstream media took an upbeat tone toward the World Cup despite perceptions that the South Korean team was playing "dirty" and getting away with it.[25] Disgruntled, many Japanese (particularly those with nationalistic views) took their opinions online, where they could express them without the constraints of official policy or political correctness.[26] The far right still influences the Japanese political landscape today, which has led some to argue that center-right political parties risk "developing into a far right, xenophobic political force."[27]

Despite the growing influence of technology on information propagation and consumption, the mechanisms, methods, and potential results—both positive and negative—are still poorly understood. Any event that receives global attention, whether an election or a megaevent, such as the Olympics, is likely to attract cyber propaganda in various forms, some which may have significant negative consequences.[28]

---

[23] Trend Micro, "Security Predictions: The Next Tier," December 6, 2016.

[24] Furuya Tsunehira, "The Roots and Realities of Japan's Cyber-Nationalism," Sasakawa Peace Foundation USA, January 29, 2016.

[25] Will Magee, "How the 2002 World Cup Became the Most Controversial Tournament in Recent Memory," *Vice Sports*, July 18, 2017; Franklin Foer, "The Man Who Ruined the World Cup," *Slate*, June 28, 2002.

[26] Tsunehira, 2016.

[27] Jiro Yamaguchi, "Signs of the Far Right in Japan's Politics," *Japan Times*, August 29, 2017.

[28] Trend Micro, 2016.

Snapshot Review of the Cybersecurity Landscape: Important Trends to Consider in the Run-Up to the Tokyo 2020 Olympics

As we have discussed, a number of threats characterize the Japanese cybersecurity threat landscape. In particular, there are four high-level threat categories to prioritize in the run-up to Tokyo 2020:

1. **Targeted attacks**, aimed at high-profile Olympic assets, individuals, or organizations (e.g. broadcasting systems, Olympic commissioners, Japanese cybersecurity organizations), for either financial or political gain, could result in severe breaches or financial or reputational losses.

2. **DDoS attacks** against Tokyo 2020 infrastructure or associated networks could disrupt the availability of services or distract from other ongoing attacks. DDoS attacks could be launched by advanced threat actors, such as nation-states, or less sophisticated groups, such as hacktivists.[29] Particular attention should be paid to developments in DDoS methods, including IoT-powered botnets.

3. **Ransomware attacks** could affect a wide range of devices, services, and underlying infrastructure supporting the Tokyo 2020 Olympics, including participant and visitor devices, transportation services, and point-of-sale systems.

4. **Cyber propaganda or misinformation** could be deployed to cause reputational loss for individuals, sponsor organizations, or the host nation. It could also be deployed for political purposes or to disrupt the Olympic Games themselves.

---

[29] *Hacktivist* is a portmanteau of *hacker* and *activist*.

CHAPTER FOUR

Lessons from Prior Olympic Games

This chapter presents an overview of cybersecurity challenges and lessons identified from earlier Olympic Games. We investigated the available open-source literature on Rio 2016, London 2012, and the Vancouver 2010 Winter Olympic Games. Sources of information on cybersecurity planning, incidents, and lessons learned included contemporary news reports, government and private-sector reports, and published interviews with cybersecurity subject-matter experts who supported the games' planning.

This chapter draws lessons from prior Olympic Games that Japan's cybersecurity policy community—including government, critical national infrastructure, and industry stakeholders—can apply in preparing for the cybersecurity threat landscape of Tokyo 2020. These findings, along with the risk assessment of the Tokyo 2020 cybersecurity landscape detailed in Chapter Five, should contribute meaningfully to current debates on cybersecurity policy options in advance of the games.

Vancouver 2010 Winter Olympic Games

In July 2003, the International Olympic Committee selected Vancouver as the host city for the 2010 Winter Olympic Games. The February 12–28, 2010, games hosted 2,566 athletes from 82 countries. The games also drew around 18,500 volunteers and nearly 10,000 media representatives (broadcast, online, and print).[1] The Canadian government quickly identified cybersecurity as a core area of concern for Vancouver 2010, as the scale and profile of the games made them for a rich target for potential cybercriminals, hacktivists, and other actors. Although experts acknowledged the risks of data theft and DoS attacks, the primary concerns related the potential reputational damage hacktivist and criminal activity could inflict on Canada's brand "with all eyes on Canada" during the games.[2]

The Canadian government incorporated cybersecurity into broader planning and exercises for Vancouver 2010 and established a cybersecurity steering committee. The Cyber Security Working Group—under the auspices of the steering committee and chaired by Public Safety Canada and the Royal Canadian Mounted Police—helped incorporate cyber incidents into two of three large-scale Olympic exercises (Silver and Gold) run by the National Exercise Division of Public Safety Canada. Exercise Gold involved 140 agencies, 45 coordination centers, and 2,000 participants.[3]

Beginning in July 2009, a small Defence Research and Development Canada (DRDC) team conducted a six-month cybersecurity review to provide recommendations to the Vancouver games' Integrated Security Unit and the Canadian Computer Incident Response Centre (CCIRC), the national center for cyber-based threats to critical infrastructure.[4] The DRDC team developed a cyber threat and risk assessment with cyber intelligence experts and then reviewed it with key cyber stakeholders to identify potential solutions and mini-

---

[1]   International Olympic Committee, "The Winter Olympic Games," factsheet, September 2014.

[2]   Luc Beaudoin and Lynne Genik, *Review and Coordination of Cyber Security for Vancouver 2010*, Ottawa, Canada: Defence Research and Development Canada Centre for Security Science, 2010, p. 2.

[3]   Robert Pitcher, cyber incident handler, Public Safety Canada, "Vancouver 2010 Olympics Lessons Learned: Cyber," presentation at the FIRST Conference, Vienna, Austria, June 15, 2011.

[4]   DRDC is an agency of Canada's Department of National Defence that conducts military science and technology-related research for the department, the Canadian Armed Forces, and other national security and public safety agencies.

mize risk. DRDC sought to determine whether cybersecurity stake-holders were applying best practices by asking them to complete the Asset Management, Communications and Operations Management, and Access Control sections of the Information Security Management ISO/IEC 17799:2005 Audit Checklist.[5] The team also assessed incident response capabilities across key stakeholders and took steps to improve monitoring and response capabilities for Vancouver 2010 by establishing standard operating procedures for incident response and promoting information sharing in advance of the games.[6] Finally, the team assessed how to fulfill information exchange requirements and identified ISP-critical dependencies.[7]

The DRDC cybersecurity review identified several issues to address in the lead-up to Vancouver 2010: (1) gaps in Canada's cyber threat situational awareness, (2) siloed planning for cybersecurity threats and responses, and (3) agencies' lack of a coordinated response capability.[8] The DRDC team found that information sharing and cross-stakeholder collaboration would be key challenges (given the limited time remaining before the games). Therefore, it proposed that the CCIRC—already the national center for cyber-based threats to critical infrastructure—serve as the key facilitator and convener for the games' cybersecurity community. Beginning a few weeks before the Olympic Games and continuing through the Paralympic Games, CCIRC convened regular, brief teleconferences among key stakeholders to share information and build trust.

---

[5] The International Organization for Standardization (ISO) and the International Electrotechnical Commission (IEC) publish the Information Security Management ISO/IEC 17799:2005, a "code of practice" for information security management.

[6] For example, the team shared contact and capability information through service desks and network operations centers and also established "information sharing of traffic monitoring at stakeholder gateways in advance of the Games to pick up reconnaissance attempts or emerging threats" (Beaudoin and Genik, 2010, pp. 2–3).

[7] Beaudoin and Genik, 2010, pp. 2–3.

[8] Lynne Genik and Luc Beaudoin, Defense Research and Development Canada and Canada Cyber Incident Response Centre, "Cyber Security Information Sharing: A Case Study of Olympic Proportions," presentation at the CRHNet Symposium, Vancouver, Canada, October 24, 2012.

Outcomes and Lessons Identified

Going into Vancouver 2010, the Canadian government was most concerned about the potential reputational effects of hacktivist activities and criminal exploitation of Olympics-related cyber infrastructure. On the whole, however, malicious cyber activity during the 2010 Vancouver Olympic Games was relatively limited. Nevertheless, stakeholders did report some activities to CCIRC, including the following:

- A spoofed copy of the Vancouver Organising Committee's website,[9] hosted in Ukraine, distributed a video containing codec malware.[10] The committee and CCIRC collaborated to take down the Ukrainian site.
- The Vancouver Organising Committee identified search engine optimization poisoning that used Olympic themes and was being used to direct users to websites that distributed malware. CCIRC issued a cybersecurity awareness bulletin in response.
- Stakeholders reported a number of minor virus infections that were remediated locally (however, cross-organizational support was offered when required).[11]

A key cybersecurity lesson from Vancouver 2010 is that building relationships and trust among public- and private-sector stakeholders is essential: Joint or collaborative cybersecurity efforts should take into account the fact that there is "no clear national owner of the cybersecurity puzzle."[12] The DRDC team found that "identifying key stakeholders, building trust amongst them, and providing an information sharing forum was an efficient and effective way to mitigate cyber risks."[13] For example, regular communication and information sharing

---

[9]   The fraudulent website contained an additional "u" (www.vaucouver2010.com); the correct address was www.vancouver2010.com.

[10]   A codec is a program that allows video storage, transmission, and playback by encoding and decoding digital data streams.

[11]   Beaudoin and Genik, 2010, pp. 10–11; Genik and Beaudoin, 2012, p. 21.

[12]   Beaudoin and Genik, 2010, p. 12.

[13]   Genik and Beaudoin, 2012, p. 22.

among key stakeholders enabled a "rapid deconfliction of 'cyber attack' reports, such as misinterpretation of the [search engine optimization] poisoning events as actual attacks on the Games' IT infrastructure."[14] While the Vancouver 2010 cybersecurity planners would have benefited greatly from more lead time, their decision to concentrate their limited time and resources on relationship- and trust-building efforts appears to have resulted in improved outcomes.

London 2012 Olympic Games

In July 2005, the International Olympic Committee voted to select London for the 2012 Summer Olympic Games. The July 27–August 12, 2012, games drew 10,568 athletes from 204 countries.[15] Dubbed the first digital Olympic Games, they were the first Summer Olympics to take place in the smartphone era and saw unprecedented use of Wi-Fi and mobile services (including the world's largest high-density Wi-Fi network, installed by BT and Cisco around Olympic Park).[16] London 2012 planners recognized the potential reputational risks and hostile threats associated with cybersecurity, and they incorporated these concerns into planning earlier in the process than the Vancouver 2010 planners.[17]

London 2012 undertook a multipronged cybersecurity strategy that included a 30-point cybersecurity action plan.[18] Key cybersecurity efforts to highlight include the following:

---

[14] Beaudoin and Genik, 2010, pp. 10–11; Genik and Beaudoin, 2012, p. 21.

[15] International Olympic Committee, "The Games of the Olympiad," factsheet, January 2017.

[16] Oliver Hoare, UK Home Office, "London 2012: Cyber Security," presentation slides, undated.

[17] Oliver Hoare (2012, p. 7) highlights threats posed by cybercrime, cyberespionage (APTs), cyberterrorism, and hacktivism.

[18] Hoare, 2012, p. 8.

- The Olympic Cyber Co-ordination Team, the first "Olympic CERT," brought together representatives from the Home Office, Ministry of Defence, Security Service/MI5, Cyber Security Operations Centre, Government Communication Headquarters, and Centre for the Protection of National Infrastructure.
- The Technology Operations Centre, operated around the clock by the London Organising Committee's IT team, was jointly staffed by BT, Atos, and Cisco and had secure, direct communication lines to the Olympic Cyber Co-ordination Team.
- Critical systems experts used a combination of inspections, visits, questionnaires, and "games readiness statements" to review roughly 450 systems and identify 40 that were critical to the successful execution of London 2012. The criteria included the systems' importance for public safety, a given sporting event, the ability to broadcast and the quality of the transmission, the spectator's experience, and the UK's reputation.[19]
- Testing and war-gaming exercises incorporating cyber, such as Flaming Torch (tabletop exercises), Bending Metal (specific to cyber and CERT testing), and command post exercises (fully integrated testing), were employed to identify and test key assumptions and reaction times.[20]
- Police operations, for example, Operation Podium, targeted illegal ticket sales online.
- Engagement with key stakeholders from government, industry, sponsors and broadcasters, transportation and public utilities, and the general public further expanded the London Organising Committee's ability to harvest information, respond quickly, gain

---

[19] Hoare, 2012, p. 15. In 2011, Gerry Pennell said of London 2012's IT infrastructure,

We keep mission-critical components quite separated from externally facing systems. . . . We use a content delivery network to push out data, which makes it hard for us to be hit by a denial of service attack because our front end is highly distributed. (In Bryan Glick, "CIO Interview: Gerry Pennell, CIO, London 2012 Olympics," *Computer Weekly*, October 14, 2011)

[20] Hoare, 2012, p. 15.

buy-in, build trust, disseminate information, and head off cyber threats before they could metastasize.

Outcomes and Lessons Identified

Overall, London 2012's cybersecurity efforts were considered a success, and they games saw only low-level cybersecurity incidents. There were no successful high-profile, high-impact events. Of an estimated 165 million "security-related events," the 2012 Olympics chief information officer (CIO), Gerry Pennell, reported that 97 were serious enough to be referred to the Technology Operations Centre, and only six would have had a major operational impact on the games.[21] Pennell described some of these major cyberattacks:

- On July 26 (the day before the games opened), a high-profile group of Eastern European hackers probed London 2012's IT infrastructure for roughly ten minutes. The group has a history of publishing the vulnerabilities of high-profile websites; however, in this case, "they didn't find anything," and no vulnerabilities were published.[22]
- July 27 saw a massive 40-minute DDoS attack on the Olympic Park's power systems starting at around 5:00 p.m., with an estimated 10 million requests originating from 90 IP addresses in North American and Europe. This automated botnet-style attack failed and was likely intended to disrupt the opening ceremony.[23] Government Communication Headquarters had forewarned London 2012 officials of a potential cyber threat to the park's

---

[21] Speaking at a cybersecurity event in 2013, Pennell said,

> There were 165 million security-related events. Most of those, let's be clear, were trivial—password changes, logon failures and things of that nature, but there were 97 actual security incidents that got raised to my technology operations center. . . . [And] only six made it to the top, to me as CIO responsible for the technology of the Olympics. (In Graeme Burton, "How the London Olympics Dealt with Six Major Cyber Attacks," *Computing*, March 6, 2013; omission in original)

[22] Burton, 2013.

[23] Burton, 2013.

power systems that morning, and the officials had tried to remediate the threat.[24]

- Beginning on July 28 and continuing over the course of four to five days, hacktivists took to social media with a call to "#letthegamesbegin." They urged individuals to pool resources to mount timed DoS attacks against the London 2012 IT infrastructure. These threats and publicly coordinated efforts had virtually no impact.[25]

- On an unspecified date, there was a "serious 330,000 packet per second DDoS on one of the IP addresses as part of our service to press agencies."[26]

- Additionally, it was reported in multiple media outlets that there was a suspected state-sponsored cyberattack.[27]

Describing the threat to the Olympic Park's power systems during the opening ceremony, the former head of London 2012 cybersecurity, Oliver Hoare, said, "If the lights had gone off during the opening ceremony, with close to a billion people watching, the impact would have been enormous." By the time the ceremony began, London 2012 officials were confident that they could recover from any loss of power within 30 seconds, but as Hoare stated, "Thirty seconds at the opening ceremony with the lights going down would have been catastrophic in terms of reputational hit."[28]

---

[24] Gordon Corera, "The 'Cyber-Attack' Threat to London's Olympic Ceremony," BBC News, July 8, 2013.

[25] Burton, 2013.

[26] Matthew Finnegan, "Olympics Was Targeted by State-Sponsored Cyber Attack, Says LOCOG CIO," *Computer World UK*, November 20, 2013.

[27] About this attack, CIO Pennell stated,

> There was also something that looked suspiciously like a state attack that happened about six days into the Games. Happily, we had been advised in the past that something like this might happen and we made some configuration changes on the Akamai piece which fielded that, but another agency did get affected. (In Finnegan, 2013)

[28] In Corera, 2013.

Other low-level cyber-related activities or incidents during London 2012 included laptop thefts, thefts of high-value IT and communication equipment, spoof websites and email scams (e.g., selling fake tickets), a virus that affected construction (Conficker), and DoS and DDoS attacks on the official Olympics website and UK government and sponsor websites.[29]

The general success of London 2012 makes it a valuable source of cybersecurity lessons for Japan 2020. Former London 2012 cybersecurity head Oliver Hoare identified "what [London 2012] got right" on cybersecurity:

- testing and exercises to ensure cybersecurity preparedness
- contributions by the Olympic CERT—the Olympic Cyber Coordination Team—to command, control, and communication capabilities (though it would have been better if a UK CERT had been in place beforehand)
- allocating resources ahead of time
- cooperating with industry partners, such as BT, Cisco, and Atos
- coordinating and collaborating with broadcasting organizations (subject to critical threats) and utilities (subject to low-level threats with a potentially high impact).[30]

Hoare also identified key lessons and areas for improvement:

- Understand that ICT is very expensive, particularly when it must be retrofit. The lesson is to aim to get it right first time and ensure that cybersecurity considerations are accounted for even in the requirements and procurement stages.
- Start planning early so that it is possible to build in cybersecurity and information assurance from very beginning, preferably in the contract phase; establish senior leadership and governance earlier; and engage sooner with ministers and other government leadership.

---

[29] Hoare, 2012.

[30] Hoare, 2012, p. 18.

- Build relationships with commercial providers and government early.
- Coordinate across many different systems and sectors (via the Information Assurance and Cyber Security Coordination Group/ Senior ICT Group/Olympic Cyber Coordination Team). This step is difficult but crucial to successfully detecting and mitigating cybersecurity threats.
- Consider cyber incidents and issues in insurance terms. For example, what will it cost if media outlets lose the ability to broadcast?[31]

Rio 2016 Olympic Games

In October 2009, the International Olympic Committee selected Rio de Janeiro as the host city for the 2016 Summer Olympics. The August 5–21, 2016, games drew 11,237 athletes from 205 countries.[32] Before and during the games, international media widely publicized cyber-related threats to the Olympics and attendees.[33] Analysis showed that Rio 2016 did face a wide range of cyber-related threats, several of which were described in a May 2016 Booz Allen Hamilton study:

- cybercrime, such as ATM card skimming and point-of-sale malware that can capture and duplicate credit and debit card information
- scams, for example, fraudulent ticket sales for Olympics-related events, as well as fake websites used to collect and steal payment credentials and PII

---

[31] Hoare, 2012, pp. 18–19.

[32] International Olympic Committee, 2017.

[33] Chris Francescani, "Brazil Superhackers Stalk Olympic Tourists," NBC News, August 11, 2016; Chris Morris, "Experts Warn of Hacking Threat at Rio Olympics," CNBC, July 19, 2016; Lucian Constantin, "Cybercrime Infrastructure Being Ramped Up in Brazil Ahead of Olympics," *PCWorld*, August 1, 2016.

- fake Wi-Fi networks—some disguised as official Rio 2016 networks—used to collect and steal PII or the exploitation of unsecured Wi-Fi networks
- exploitation of online payment systems, which facilitated the theft of credentials and PII to convert funds into Boletos, a payment method used widely in Brazil, as well as the use of Boleto malware commit fraud
- hacktivist activity in response to budget overruns during the 2014 FIFA World Cup that saw a resurgence in the months leading up to Rio 2016.[34]

The Brazilian Network Information Center (NIC.br) is the executive branch of the Brazilian Internet Steering Committee and maintains the Brazilian National Computer Emergency Response Team (CERT.br). During Rio 2016, NIC.br and CERT.br were responsible for identifying potential threats and needs related to infrastructure and processes; collecting and monitoring incidents reported by stakeholders; monitoring networks and data feeds for defacement or intrusions, including public sources of information, such as social media and public-facing websites; facilitating communication and coordination among various stakeholders, particularly CSIRTs, telecommunications companies, ISPs, hosting companies, and international partners; training incident handling teams; and maintaining the Inter-Network Operations Centre Dial-by-ASN (more commonly known as INOC-DBA), a VoIP network that enables communication among network operations centers, security incident response teams, and other essential personnel.[35]

---

[34] Booz Allen and Cyber4Sight, *2016 Rio Summer Olympic Games Cyberthreat Environment*, May 26, 2016. Examples of hacktivist activity included Anonymous Brazil publicizing the hashtag #OpOlympicHacking; in February 2016, it claimed to have breached Brazilian petroleum company Petrobras, its online supplier portal Petronect, and the consulting firm Accenture and leaked PII for more than 1,000 employees. In April that year, it claimed responsibility for a DDoS attack on Brazil's national telecommunications agency, Anatel. The following month, it called for a DDoS attack against the domain brasil2016.gov.br.

[35] Lucimara Desiderá, CERT.br, "Lessons Learned from the Rio2016 Summer Olympic Games," presentation at the San José FIRST Technical Colloquium, San José, Costa Rica, September 2016b, slide. 5.

In total, four teams collaborated to prevent, identify, and respond to cyber incidents during Rio 2016:

- Rio2016 CSIRT provided round-the-clock onsite support and handled incidents related to the Rio 2016 infrastructure, phishing attempts targeting official Rio 2016 websites, and websites selling fake tickets.
- CERT.br coordinated and facilitated communication with external stakeholders, provided situational awareness, and conducted network monitoring. Incident reporters were encouraged to copy CERT.br on any notifications to Rio2016 CSIRT to support situational awareness.
- CTIR Gov, a Brazilian governmental CSIRT, handled incidents that targeted networks belonging to the Brazilian Federal Public Administration.
- Centre for Cyber Defence personnel staffed Rio 2016 security command and control centers on a continuous basis, focusing on the defense of critical infrastructure and networks of interest to the Brazilian Ministry of Defence.[36]

Outcomes and Lessons Identified

Due to the high level of cybercrime in Brazil and ever-increasing ICT requirements for successive Olympic Games, Rio 2016 faced a greater cybersecurity challenge than either London 2012 or Vancouver 2010. Despite these challenges, there were no high-profile, high-impact cyber incidents that negatively affected Rio's ICT infrastructure. Rio 2016 cybersecurity planners applied lessons learned from the 2014 World Cup, seeking engagement and commitment from the local organizing committee and establishing Rio2016 CSIRT as a round-the-clock focal point for notifications.[37] Nonetheless, Rio2016 CSIRT and CERT.br

---

[36] Desiderá, 2016b, p. 6.

[37] Lucimara Desiderá, CERT.br, "Incident Handling in High Profile International Events: Lessons Learned and the Road Ahead," presentation at the FIRST/TF-CSIRT Technical Colloquium Prague, Czech Republic, January 2016a; Desiderá, 2016b, p. 7.

did identify, observe, or respond to a number of lower-level incidents, including

- cybercriminals' exploitation of the games to attract financial fraud victims
- unauthorized ticket selling on fake websites
- hacktivism, including website defacements, although at a much lower level than during the 2014 FIFA World Cup
- data leaks from government and Olympics-related organizations (e.g., the World Anti-Doping Agency)[38]
- DDoS attacks against government and Olympic sponsors' websites, peaking at 300–500 Gbps.[39]

In a post–Olympic Games review of cybersecurity efforts, a CERT.br expert identified three categories of lessons:

1. "Cooperation is everything." Clearly defining and dividing core responsibilities, as well as promoting information sharing— even among competing vendors—is key and enables all stakeholders to work together in pursuit of a common goal.
2. "Documentation is extremely necessary." The specific tool or repository used does not matter, but a centralized means (such as a wiki) of documenting and sharing information and, especially, processes and procedures is essential.
3. Simulations and training should be nonstop, incorporate wargames and live rehearsals, and build a community of practice and stakeholders.[40]

---

[38] In some cases, it was not possible to verify the authenticity of the data.

[39] Desiderá, 2016b, pp. 9–10.

[40] Desiderá, 2016b, pp. 14–16.

Summary of Lessons Identified

As Olympic organizers' reliance on ICT infrastructure has steadily increased over successive Olympic Games, so too have cybersecurity requirements. Despite a proliferation of adversary capabilities, the Olympic Games have yet to suffer a successful high-impact, high-profile cyberattack.[41] Based on the relative success of Olympic cybersecurity planners so far, we identified five general categories of lessons for Tokyo 2020:

1. **Plan early** so there is sufficient time to assess event-specific threats, build trust and a community of stakeholders, and establish mechanisms and processes for information sharing, incident reporting, and problem resolution.
2. **Prioritize cooperation and information sharing**, particularly by drawing in private-sector stakeholders, recognizing that there is no single owner or stakeholder in Olympic cybersecurity.
3. **Create a shared mission and common cybersecurity goal** to help bolster trust and individual stakeholders' openness and commitment to information sharing.
4. **Establish clear roles and responsibilities among stakeholders** to help them understand how to support the common goal and respond to specific challenges.
5. **Incorporate cybersecurity** into broader security planning, training, and exercises right from the start.

These lessons can offer key insights for cybersecurity planners when overlaid with the unique cybersecurity threat landscape of Tokyo 2020.

---

[41] Numerous cyberattacks have targeted Olympic infrastructure, attendees, participants, and VIPs since 2010. For example, a 40-minute DDoS attack on July 27, 2012, failed to take down the Olympic Park's power systems during the Opening Ceremony. The 2016 Rio games saw cybercriminals defrauding victims, as well as data leaks from government and Olympics-related organizations; however, these attacks did not directly target Olympic ICT infrastructure.

CHAPTER FIVE

A Risk Assessment of Japan's Cybersecurity Landscape

This chapter presents a risk assessment of the Tokyo 2020 cybersecurity landscape. The principles, framework, and processes of the risk assessment were adopted from the international standard and principles for risk management (ISO 31000).[1] We synthesized the qualitative and quantitative data reported earlier in this report (i.e., the threat landscape analysis in Chapter Three and lessons from prior Olympics in Chapter Four), as well as our review of the academic literature and data from two interviews with Japanese cybersecurity subject-matter experts. The result is a prioritized threat actor typology, which considers the level of sophistication and motivation of threat actors likely to be operating in the Tokyo 2020 threat landscape.

Overview of the Risk Management Process

We adapted an existing risk assessment framework—the ISO/IEC 31000 family of standards—to assess the risks faced by Tokyo 2020. Risk management can help organizations achieve their security goals and objectives by identifying opportunities and threats, as well as by helping them effectively allocate limited resources to mitigate risk. The process comprises a number of steps, shown in Figure 5.1:

---

[1] ISO provides principles and generic guidelines on risk management in its 31000 series of documents. The principles and guidelines can be used by any public, private, or community enterprise; association; group; or individual. They are not specific to any industry or sector.

Figure 5.1
Overview of the Risk Management Process

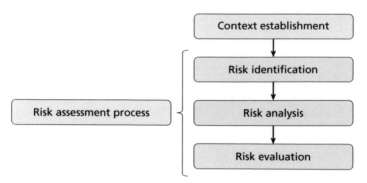

SOURCE: Adapted from ISO, "ISO 31000:2009, Risk Management," webpage, undated.

- Context establishment occurs first. It involves setting the scope, boundaries, and goals for the information risk management process.
- Risk assessment follows context establishment and incorporates three processes to identify, analyze, and evaluate risks:
  - Risk identification determines what harm could occur to an asset. It requires the development of insight into how, where, and why this harm could occur.
  - Risk analysis determines the likelihood and potential impact of a particular threat actor—and assigns a value to it.
  - Risk evaluation prioritizes and ranks threat actors according to the risk analysis criteria. Risk evaluations and risk analysis help actors make decisions about the best course of action.

A Cybersecurity Goal Must Be Established Prior to a Risk Analysis

Setting a cybersecurity goal is necessary for conducting a risk analysis like the one described here. Once the context has been established and a cybersecurity goal has been defined, a risk-based assessment can be conducted.[2]

> Cybersecurity goal: To maintain the safety, security, integrity, functionality, and accessibility of information technology systems of importance to Tokyo 2020, with due care and consideration of IT-related risks to the games, partners, and related businesses.

Cyber threats are broadly defined as anything that could constitute tampering, destruction, or interruption of any IT service or that could have an adverse effect on the cybersecurity goal. According to the literature on information security risk management, a cybersecurity goal is typically underpinned by four IT security objectives: confidentiality, integrity, availability, and accountability.[3]

- *Confidentiality* refers to the protection of data from intentional or unintentional attempts to access it by unauthorized users. Confidentiality covers data in storage, during processing, and in transit.
- *Integrity* refers to the prevention of either intentional or accidental attempts to add to, delete, manipulate, or otherwise alter data or data management systems.
- *Availability* refers to the need to protect data against intentional or accidental unauthorized deletion or other DoS incidents or theft.
- *Accountability* at the individual level refers to the traceability of events to a unique entity. Assigning accountability is an organizational policy requirement for implementing other procedures, such as nonrepudiation (ensuring that a party cannot deny an action), deterrence, fault isolation (determining the type and location of an error or issue), intrusion detection and prevention, and post-incident analysis and legal action.[4]

---

[2]   The NIST special publication on computer security gives a relevant definition of an *information technology security goal*, which we have adapted to the context of Japan's cybersecurity landscape: Gary Stoneburner, *Underlying Technical Models for Information Technology Security*, National Institute of Standards and Technology, SP 800-33, December 2001 (withdrawn on August 1, 2018).

[3]   Stoneburner, 2001.

[4]   Stoneburner, 2001.

These four security objectives are interdependent, as shown in Figure 5.2. All security objectives are required for information assurance, which is the basis for measuring confidence that security measures are effective, both technically and operationally, and work as intended. For Tokyo 2020, IT systems must reach an acceptable level of assurance relative to the risks faced by those systems. A high assurance level not only encourages confidence in the security of systems, but it also minimizes the risk of undesirable actions.

Identifying Threat Actors and Hacker Typologies

The threat actors of interest in this study were those individuals or groups that might seek to compromise the cybersecurity goal of the Tokyo 2020 Olympics or any of its constituent IT security objectives. After reviewing the relevant literature, identified through the rapid evidence assessment method (as explained in Appendix A), we appropriated existing hacker typologies and applied them to the context of Tokyo 2020, as described in Box 5.1. We list the identified actors in Table 5.1, which also describes their recent operations that are relevant to Japan's cybersecurity threat landscape.

Figure 5.2
Cybersecurity Interdependencies

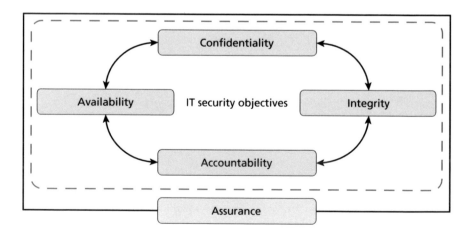

We found that the typologies developed by Markus K. Rogers and Ryan Seebruck captured the most relevant analytical categories for collecting and organizing the data of interest to our study. Table 5.1 lists six categories of cyber threat actors active in the Japanese cybersecurity landscape with the potential to pose challenges to cybersecurity planners in the lead-up to Tokyo 2020 or after the games have begun.

Box 5.1
The Existing Literature on Hacker Typologies

Typologies are useful because they allow researchers and security planners to classify threat actors into ideal types, rather than exhaustive listings, to understand the risk landscape and attendant threats.[a]

Marcus Rogers at Purdue University has generated a detailed list of hacker types that has enhanced understanding of the hacker community and various hacker subtypes.[b] Although there was not one generic profile of a hacker, Rogers identified at least eight subclassifications: novices, cyberpunks, internals, petty thieves, virus writers, old-guard hackers, professional criminals, and information warriors. In one study, Rogers analyzed the self-reported criminal behavior of hackers to produce a psychological analysis of the subjects.[c]

Ryan Seebruck at the University of Arizona employed Rogers's taxonomy and further explored the rise of socially and ideologically motivated hacking as he constructed his own typology. Seebruck's work contributed to scholarship in this field by visually representing multiple motivations (e.g., profit, ideology, prestige, recreation, revenge) simultaneously.[d]

[a] Kevin B. Smith, "Typologies, Taxonomies, and the Benefits of Policy Classification," *Policy Studies Journal*, Vol. 30, No. 3, August 2002.

[b] Marcus K. Rogers, "A Two-Dimensional Circumplex Approach to the Development of a Hacker Taxonomy," *Digital Investigation*, Vol. 3, No. 2, June 2006.

[c] Marcus K. Rogers, Kathryn Seigfried, and Kirti Tidke, "Self-Reported Computer Criminal Behavior: A Psychological Analysis," *Digital Investigation*, Vol. 3, Supplement, September 2006.

[d] Ryan Seebruck, "A Typology of Hackers: Classifying Cyber Malfeasance Using a Weighted Arc Circumplex Model," *Digital Investigation*, Vol. 14, September 2015.

Table 5.1
Threat Actor Identification in the Japanese Cybersecurity Landscape

Threat Actor	Definition
Cybercriminals/ organized crime	The definition of *organized criminal group* is adapted from Article 2 of the United Nations Convention on Transnational Organized Crime, which describes "a structured group of three or more persons, existing for a period of time and acting in concert with the aim of committing one or more serious crimes or offences . . . to obtain, directly or indirectly, a financial or other material benefit."[a] *Cybercriminals with links to North Korea have targeted Japan and other nations with the WannaCry malware scam.*
Insider threats	An insider threat is a class of individuals who use their knowledge or access privileges to exploit network vulnerabilities or attack systems that they use or administer.[b] Insider threat research suggests that many perpetrators are triggered by a negative work-related experience, plan the attack in advance, mix sophisticated and unsophisticated techniques, attack remotely, and are financially motivated.[c] *A paradigmatic case of an insider threat is Chelsea Manning, the former U.S. Army soldier who furnished WikiLeaks with nearly 750,000 classified or unclassified but sensitive military and diplomatic documents.[d]*
Foreign intelligence services	Foreign intelligence services are highly capable nation-state organizations that can deploy considerable resources to threaten the cybersecurity goals of Tokyo 2020. They have the capability to intercept data, influence other threat actors to steal data, and hack into networks for industrial espionage or other purposes. Attribution of state-sponsored cyberespionage capabilities, cybercrime groups, and offensive cyberattacks is often difficult because of a reliance on widely available tools, techniques, and procedures. *APTs assumed to be working under the direction or at the behest of foreign countries have allegedly targeted Japan in the past and will likely continue to operate in Japan's threat landscape. Several hacking groups and APTs (e.g., Lazarus Group and APT1) have implicit and speculative connections to potentially hostile and adversarial states, including China, North Korea, and Russia.*
Hacktivists	Digital protestors and activists, otherwise known as hacktivists when they take their political views into cyberspace, emerged in the mid-1990s and engaged in hacking activities with an overt political stance.[e] *The group Anonymous has a long history of conducting operations against Olympic Games host nations, as demonstrated at London 2012 and Rio 2016.*

Table 5.1—Continued

Threat Actor	Definition
Cyberterrorists	Terrorism, and, by extension, cyberterrorism, is defined as an action that endangers or causes serious violence to a person or people, causes serious damage to property, or seriously interferes or disrupts an electronic system.[f] The use or threat of violence is designed to influence the government or intimidate the public with the intent to advance a political, religious, or ideological cause. Historical acts of terrorism continue to shape the security agenda for the Olympics, and terror attacks have targeted the games in the past, including Munich 1972 and Atlanta 1996.[g] More recently, terrorist groups have used social media platforms to radicalize and recruit new members, provide instruction in tactics and weapons, gather intelligence about potential targets, communicate clandestinely, and support terrorist operations.[h]
Ticket scalpers	Ticket scalpers use "bots" and computer programs to automate the process of buying a ticket from a legitimate ticket seller and re-selling it for a highly inflated price.[i] Ticket scalpers have operated at many successive Olympic Games, as described in Chapter Four.

[a] United Nations Office on Drugs and Crime, *United Nations Convention Against Transnational Organized Crime and the Protocols Thereto*, 2004.

[b] Eric D Shaw, "The Role of Behavioral Research and Profiling in Malicious Cyber Insider Investigations," *Digital Investigation*, Vol. 3, No. 1, March 2006, p. 21.

[c] Marissa Reddy Randazzo, Michelle Keeney, Eileen Kowalski, Dawn Cappelli, and Andrew Moore, *Insider Threat Study: Illicit Cyber Activity in the Banking and Finance Sector*, Pittsburgh, Pa.: Software Engineering Institute, Carnegie Mellon University, June 2005.

[d] Chelsea Manning, "The Years Since I Was Jailed for Releasing the 'War Diaries' Have Been a Rollercoaster," *The Guardian*, May 27, 2015.

[e] Tim Jordan and Paul A Taylor, *Hacktivism and Cyberwars: Rebels with a Cause?* New York: Routledge, 2004, p. 12.

[f] Ines Von Behr, Anais Reding, Charlie Edwards, and Luke Gribbon, *Radicalisation in the Digital Era: The Use of the Internet in 15 Cases of Terrorism and Extremism*, Santa Monica, Calif.: RAND Corporation, 2013.

[g] Ramón Spaaij, "Terrorism and Security at the Olympics: Empirical Trends and Evolving Research Agendas," *International Journal of the History of Sport*, Vol. 33, No. 4, February 2016.

[h] Examples include al Qaeda and the Islamic State and their affiliates. See Brian Michael Jenkins, *Is Al Qaeda's Internet Strategy Working?* testimony before the Counterterrorism and Intelligence Subcommittee, Homeland Security Committee, U.S. House of Representatives, Santa Monica, Calif.: RAND Corporation, CT-371, 2011.

[i] Jason Koebler, "The Man Who Broke Ticketmaster," *Motherboard*, February 10, 2017; Ben Sisario, "Congress Moves to Curb Ticket Scalping, Banning Bots Used Online," *New York Times*, December 8, 2016.

The Motivation and Sophistication of Threat Actors

The motivations and level of sophistication of threat actors vary depending on the class of actor. For instance, hackers can be motivated by *profit* (e.g., financial reward), *ideology* (e.g., politics, religion, nationalism), *revenge* (i.e., insider threats by disgruntled workers, larger social justice issues), or a combination of factors. We selected these three motivation categories from extant typologies, which also employ other categories—such as curiosity, notoriety, prestige, and recreation.[5] We found the three motivating factors of profit, ideology, and revenge to be sufficient to describe the behavior of the threat actors that might compromise the cybersecurity goal of Tokyo 2020, as identified in Table 5.1. Furthermore, this streamlined classification of motivations avoids adding unnecessary complexity to the typology. For instance, insider threats often exhibit similar risk characteristics, such as a negative work history, lack of social skills, sense of entitlement, and ethical flexibility.[6] These underlying motivational factors most closely align with the revenge and profit categories.

A High-Level Risk Assessment of Tokyo 2020

As discussed earlier, the structure of the risk assessment adopted from the ISO/IEC 37000 standard contains three relevant processes: risk identification, risk analysis, and risk evaluation. Each of these three discrete elements of the risk assessment relies on a synthesis of data from all the sources consulted by the project team. Figure 5.3 shows the relationship between the risk assessment steps and synthesized data.

We determined the sophistication of actors by considering their previous activity within the Japanese threat landscape (discussed in Chapter Three), examining case studies of prior cybersecurity challenges at the Olympic Games (Chapter Four), and reviewing the gray literature (e.g., newspaper articles, industry threat reports, original writing by hacker groups). Table 5.2 ranks the estimated sophistication

---

[5]   Rogers, 2006; Seebruck, 2015; C. Meyers, S. Powers, and D. Faissol, *Taxonomies of Cyber Adversaries and Attacks: A Survey of Incidents and Approaches*, Livermore, Calif.: Lawrence Livermore National Laboratory, 2009.

[6]   Shaw, 2006.

Figure 5.3
Synthesized Data as Inputs for the Risk Assessment

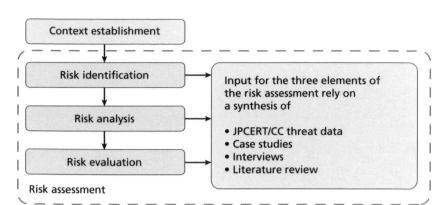

of each threat actor—low, medium, or high—based on their technical skill to conduct various types of attacks. (See Appendix C for a full
description of attack types.)

We conducted two interviews with experts in the Japanese cybersecurity policy community, guided by the interview protocol in Appendix B. These subject-matter experts provided their insights on the condition of anonymity. We asked them to prioritize the list of threat actors
and indicate a level of risk (i.e., a score of low, medium, or high, for the
parameters "likelihood" and "impact") for each of the actor classes.[7]
Ranking the threats makes the analysis more pertinent for policymakers by helping them prioritize limited resources and policy options.

Table 5.2 presents the synthesized findings from our risk assessment and each of its constituent elements. It lists the identified threat
actors, their quantified level of risk (likelihood and impact), and a risk
prioritization and threat ranking, from most to least threatening.

We synthesized data from JPCERT/CC, case studies, interviews,
and our literature review to produce the risk assessment presented in
Table 5.2. It prioritizes the threat actors who pose the greatest potential risk to cyber infrastructure and networks for Tokyo 2020 plan-

---

[7]   It should be noted that the risk levels in the "Likelihood" and "Impact" columns for particular cyber events do not necessarily shift in tandem,

Table 5.2
A Prioritized Risk Assessment of Tokyo 2020 Based on a Typology of Hackers

Threat Actor	Adversary Motivation	Sophistication	Risk Analysis			Risk Evaluation	
			Likelihood	Impact	Prioritization	Rank
Foreign intelligence services	Ideology	High	Medium	High	High	1
Cyberterrorists	Ideology/revenge	Medium	Medium	High	Medium	2
Cybercriminals/ organized crime	Profit	High	Medium	Medium	Medium	3
Hacktivists	Ideology/revenge	Medium	Medium	Medium	Medium	4
Insider threats	Revenge/profit	Medium	Low	Medium	Medium	5
Ticket scalpers	Profit	Medium	High	Low	Low	6

ners. Foreign intelligence services—should they choose to act—pose the greatest threat, with a high level of technical sophistication and the potential to have a large impact. Cyberterrorists and cybercriminals are also of concern, although less so than foreign intelligence services. Cyberterrorists have only a moderate level of technological sophistication, but their potential impact on the games could be severe. And while cybercriminals possess high levels of technical skill, we assessed both the likelihood and potential impact of these attacks as only "medium." Although they are newsworthy when they do occur, we judged attacks from hacktivists and insider threats as carrying a lower risk to the games. Finally, ticket scalpers are likely to exploit cyber vulnerabilities for profit, but their overall threat to the security of the games is low when compared with other actors.

Figure 5.4 visualizes these data, showing the sophistication, risk, and motivations of cyber threat actors with respect to the Tokyo 2020 games. The infographic provides a quick-reference visualization for Olympic security planners, CERTs, policy- and decisionmakers, and others responsible for monitoring and managing the Tokyo 2020 threat landscape.

Figure 5.4
Cyber Threats to the Tokyo 2020 Games

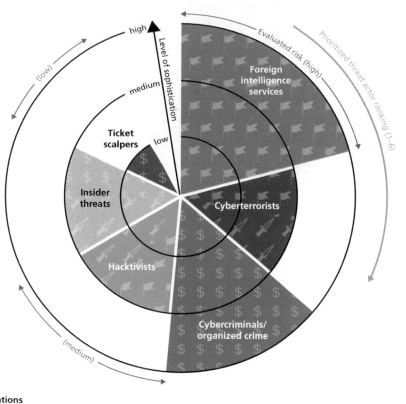

Motivations

CHAPTER SIX

Conclusions and Policy Options

The importance of cybersecurity has steadily increased over successive Olympic Games. Despite a mounting reliance on ICTs and a proliferation of adversary capabilities, the Olympic Games have yet to suffer a successful high-impact, high-profile attack. What remains to be seen is whether an adversary with the requisite sophistication, motivation, capability, and intent will conduct a successful cyber operation against a host nation in the future. To prevent and deter such an event, security planners should apportion substantial resources to effectively mitigate risk in a prioritized manner, in line with the threat rankings in Table 5.2 in Chapter Five.

This discussion of policy options is clustered around two themes: general policy options for Olympic cybersecurity planners and specific policy options related to Tokyo 2020. The general policy options are as follows:

1. **Plan early.** The earlier cybersecurity planning and preparation begins, the more time there is to assess event-specific threats, shape a community of stakeholders and build trust among them, and establish mechanisms and processes for information sharing, incident reporting, and problem resolution.
2. **Cooperate and share information.** There are a number of cybersecurity stakeholders in the public and private sectors who must collaborate, cooperate, and share information to reduce cybersecurity risks in advance of the Olympic Games. Government and Olympic planners should seek to include private-sector stakeholders in any cybersecurity cooperation and

information-sharing arrangements to effectively mitigate cyber-security risks.

3. **Know the mission and have a common security goal.** For a successful public-private, multi-stakeholder cybersecurity strategy to succeed, all parties must understand and buy into a common goal. Sharing a mission can bolster trust and increase individual stakeholders' openness and commitment to information sharing.

4. **Clearly define all stakeholder roles and responsibilities**, and revisit them throughout the preparation and execution of the games. Defining clear roles and responsibilities helps stakeholders better understand how best to contribute to the broader mission and ensures that they know to whom to refer specific challenges or incidents. For example, before the Rio 2016 games, CERT.br circulated an email identifying four key cyber teams and their responsibilities.[1]

5. **Allocate resources to mitigate cybersecurity risks.** By taking a risk-based approach to cybersecurity, we developed a prioritized list of threat actors to consider and address as part of the planning for Tokyo 2020. Effectively reducing these risks to an acceptable level will require adequate resources that are apportioned appropriately.

6. **Deter the riskiest adversaries with a targeted cyber defense campaign.** Our assessment indicated that the riskiest threat actors faced by Tokyo 2020 are foreign intelligence services (i.e., hacking groups with either implicit or explicit support from hostile foreign nation-states) and cyberterrorists (i.e., terrorist groups that use the internet to recruit and to support ICT-related terrorist attacks). Such attackers might seek to disrupt the games and embarrass the host nation. To effectively mitigate against such an event, a targeted deterrence campaign might dissuade these adversaries from attempting to attack altogether—for example, carrying out a publicly documented cybersecurity exercise to showcase defensive preparations—and convince them that the

---

[1]   Desiderá, 2016b, p. 6.

costs of executing an attack are too high, the chances of success are too low, and the prospective retaliatory costs are unbearable.

7. **Incorporate cybersecurity into broader security planning.** Planners should incorporate cybersecurity into broader security planning efforts, training, and exercises right from the start. Planners should work to build a cybersecurity community and incorporate "cyber" into the broader Olympic security community, as cyberattacks can have widespread physical security effects. For instance, Tokyo 2020 security planners could test their cyber capabilities at earlier events, such as the Rugby World Cup in 2019.

We formulated these policy options to align with the Japanese government's structures and policy apparatus (as outlined in Figure 2.1 in Chapter Two), which should be effective in achieving the cybersecurity goals of Tokyo 2020. The capability of each ministry, body, or headquarters could be further enhanced with substantial resources and by implementing the policy options presented here.

Future investigations into cybersecurity preparations for the Olympic Games could focus on the integration of cyber risks into a broader, macro-level risk model for mega-event planning. Studies could also be conducted on effective methods to deter the highest- and lowest-risk threat actors. For example, on one end of the spectrum, researchers could investigate the impact of traditional deterrence approaches through an alliance's defense posture; on the other, they could study the effectiveness of policies to temporarily introduce tougher sentencing guidelines for hacktivism and ticket scalping.

Methods

This appendix provides additional background on the study approach and an overview of the methods that we used to analyze the Japanese cybersecurity threat landscape in the lead-up to the Tokyo 2020 Olympics.

The research approach was designed around five technical work packages (WPs), with one underlying project management WP, as shown in Figure A.1. The study was designed to investigate six research objectives, which are discussed in Chapter One of this report.

WP1: "Know Thyself, Know Thy Enemy"

WP1 considered the current state of terrorist and cyber threats to Japan, as well as relevant notable cases of cyberterrorism worldwide, to inform our threat landscape profile and risk analysis. We conducted a rapid evidence assessment (REA) to accomplish Task 1.1, which also involved searching the relevant literature associated case studies. We conducted a detailed literature review on previous Olympic organizing experiences and associated cyber events—from London 2012, Rio 2016, and the Vancouver 2010 Winter Games—to identify lessons learned that could be relevant to Tokyo 2020 (Task 1.2.).

The assessment outputs totaled 45 sources on the common theme of cybersecurity challenges for Tokyo 2020. We analyzed both primary sources (e.g., peer-reviewed academic journal articles) and secondary sources (i.e., gray literature, such as editorials, newspaper articles, and

Figure A.1
Overview of the Study Approach

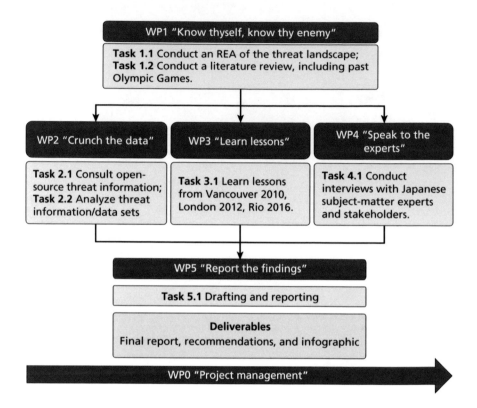

blogs) for their relevance using a keyword search. We clustered the primary literature into four broad categories using a top-down method:

- cybersecurity threats (e.g., computer hacking, cybercrime)
- terrorism literature (e.g., radicalization, cyberterrorism)
- typological studies (e.g., taxonomies and threat actor identification)
- Olympic Games literature (i.e., security at mega-events and lessons learned reviews by host nations).

Again, we used a top-down method to cluster the secondary literature into five categories:

- cybersecurity training (i.e., identifying education, training and skills gaps, shortages, and initiatives)
- industry news (e.g., press releases, market updates)
- lessons learned (i.e., relating to the UK and Brazil, sharing lessons with Japan)
- cybersecurity exercises (e.g., Japanese cyber exercises and evaluations)
- other (e.g., cybersecurity awareness, crisis management).

The output of the REA is shown in Figure A.2.

Figure A.2
Outputs of the Rapid Evidence Assessment, by Source Type and Category

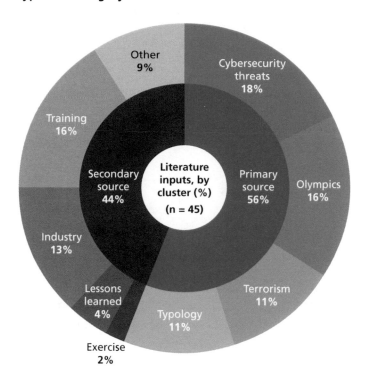

WP2: "Crunch the Data"

To complement the literature review in WP1, we conducted desktop research for WP2. We consulted open-source threat information (e.g., industry threat reports, independent security research reports) as well as threat data sets from Japanese actors (e.g., JPCERT/CC). Using a mixed-methods approach, we combined emerging findings on the cyber threat landscape from WP1 and WP2.

WP3: "Learn Lessons"

Looking at previous Olympic Games—London 2012, Rio 2016, and the Winter Olympic Games in Vancouver 2010—we considered a host of lessons learned. We focused on best practices and how prior host nations have dealt with large-scale cybersecurity challenges. We also noted where knowledge could be gained from past experiences, both successes and failures.

WP4: "Speak to the Experts"

We conducted two interviews with Japanese cybersecurity subject-matter experts who spoke with us on the condition of anonymity. The interviews were guided by the interview protocol in Appendix B, and we used these questions to solicit the experts' views and insights. We combined these findings with the outputs of WPs 1, 2, and 3 to frame the discussion in WP4.

WP5: "Report the Findings"

WP5 consisted of the synthesis, analysis, and final reporting. Here, we reviewed information captured in WPs 1, 2, 3, and 4 and developed our threat actor typology and a set of recommendations for Japanese policymakers to strengthen the country's cybersecurity posture ahead of the 2020 Olympics.

Interview Protocol

The interview protocol below was developed in advance of our interviews with Japanese stakeholders for WP4. We circulated the protocol to our subject-matter experts to solicit their insights and opinions on the questions.

The Cybersecurity Threat Landscape

1. What are the most concerning threats—in terms of either severity or prevalence—that currently shape the cybersecurity landscape?
2. What is the view of "hacking" from the perspective of the Japanese people?
3. What are the main challenges for cybersecurity policymakers and security planners in the Japanese government leading up to the 2020 Olympics?
4. How might the current geopolitical climate in the Asia-Pacific region influence the cybersecurity landscape? That is, how might tensions spill from traditional security challenges into the cyber domain?
5. To what extent do the upcoming Tokyo 2020 Olympics alter the threat landscape Japan faces?

Threat Actors

6. Which group of actors pose the largest threat to the Tokyo 2020 Games? Can you rank the threat actors in order of severity?

- contractors
- corporate intelligence
- criminals/organized crime
- disgruntled staff
- foreign intelligence services
- foreign influence campaigns
- protestors and activists
- staff undertaking unauthorized actions
- terrorists

7. Is there any indication of collusion among threat actors?
8. Are there any other threat actors that are missing?

Commitment of Resources to Address Cyber Threats

9. How does the commitment of resources (financial, personnel and training, or other) for the Olympics aim to mitigate the risk posed by the range of threat actors?
10. Are there any targeted deterrence campaigns in relation to the Olympics aimed at preventing or dissuading hackers and threat actors?

Likelihood and Impact of Events

11. Which threat actors could be the most prevalent or most likely to appear?
12. Which threat actors could have the most severe or most negative impact?
13. How might an orchestrated attack by two or more actor classes amplify or intensify the risk of a cyber incident?

Black Swan Events

14. Under what circumstances might a black swan event arise? (That is, an event that is very unlikely but would have a large impact.)

JPCERT/CC Incident Categories

Computer security incident
Any event that may occur in the management of information systems, including events that may be considered security issues or any case related to computer security.

Phishing site
A site that spoofs the legitimate site of a service provider (e.g., a bank, auction service) with the intent to obtain a user's personal information, passwords, credit card numbers, or other data for fraudulent purposes. JPCERT/CC categorizes the following as phishing sites:
- websites that imitate those of financial institutions and credit card companies
- websites that lead users to phishing sites.

Website defacement
When the contents of a website have been rewritten (including by embedding scripts not intended by the administrator) by an attacker or malware. JPCERT/CC categorizes the following as website defacement:
- websites on which an attacker or malware has embedded malicious scripts or iframes
- websites on which information has been altered as a result of an SQL (Structured Query Language) injection attack.

Malware site
A website that can infect a computer with malware when a user views the site or a website that hosts malware for an attack. JPCERT/CC categorizes the following as malware sites:

- websites that attempt to infect a visitor's computer with malware
- websites that host malware.

Scan

Unauthorized access by attackers (that does not affect the system) to search for security vulnerabilities on a server, individual computer, or any system or network targeted for an attack. Scanning could also include attempts to infect the system with malware. JPCERT/CC categorizes the following as scanning:
- vulnerability searching (e.g., checking program versions, service operation)
- attempts at intrusion that do not result in intrusion
- attempts to infect a system with malware (e.g., viruses, bots, worms) that do not result in infection
- brute-force attacks against ssh, ftp, telnet, or other protocols that do not result in a successful attack.

DoS/DDoS

An attack against the network resources of servers, computers, and other devices that form a network, resulting in an inability to provide or access services. JPCERT/CC categorizes the following as DoS/DDoS:
- attacks that exhaust network resources as a result of large number of communications
- bad responses or suspension of server programs due to a large number of requests for access
- interference of services by forcing the receipt of a large number of emails (e.g., error emails, spam).

ICS-related incident

Any incident related to an ICS. JPCERT/CC categorizes the following as ICS-related incidents:
- an attack on an ICS over the internet
- servers that communicate with malware targeting control systems
- attacks that cause the malfunctioning of an ICS.

References

Akasaka, Shinsuke, director, ICT Security Office, Japanese Ministry of Internal Affairs and Communications, "Japanese Government Cyber Security Strategy," presentation slides, January 21, 2015. As of August 1, 2018:
http://okaweb.ec.kyushu-u.ac.jp/cs/2015-0121/materials/01%20mic.pdf

Atos, "Atos Origin Reveals IT Systems for the ATHENS 2004 Olympic Games," press release, June 7, 2004.

Barker, Sara, "Japan Cybersecurity Skills Shortage in a 'State of Urgency' Before 2020 Olympics," *Security Brief Asia*, February 7, 2017. As of August 1, 2018:
https://securitybrief.asia/story/
japan-cybersecurity-skills-shortage-state-urgency-before-2020-olympics

Beaudoin, Luc, and Lynne Genik, *Review and Coordination of Cyber Security for Vancouver 2010*, Ottawa, Canada: Defense Research and Development Canada Centre for Security Science, 2010. As of August 1, 2018:
http://www.aiai.ed.ac.uk/project/coalition/ksco/ksco-2010/papers/10-04-Genik-Beaudoin-Cyber.pdf

Booz Allen Cyber4Sight, *2016 Rio Summer Olympic Games Cyberthreat Environment*, May 26, 2016. As of August 1, 2018:
https://www.boozallen.com/content/dam/boozallen_site/sig/pdf/white-paper/
cyber4sight-special-report-rio-summer-olympics.pdf

Burton, Graeme, "How the London Olympics Dealt with Six Major Cyber Attacks," *Computing*, March 6, 2013. As of August 1, 2018:
https://www.computing.co.uk/ctg/news/2252841/
how-the-london-olympics-dealt-with-six-major-cyber-attacks

Constantin, Lucian, "Cybercrime Infrastructure Being Ramped Up in Brazil Ahead of Olympics," *PCWorld*, August 1, 2016. As of August 1, 2018:
http://www.pcworld.com/article/3102991/cybercrime-infrastructure-being-ramped-up-in-brazil-ahead-of-olympics.html

Corera, Gordon, "The 'Cyber-Attack' Threat to London's Olympic Ceremony," BBC News, July 8, 2013. As of August 1, 2018:
http://www.bbc.com/news/uk-23195283

Desiderá, Lucimara, CERT.br, "Incident Handling in High Profile International Events: Lessons Learned and the Road Ahead," presentation at the FIRST/ TF-CSIRT Technical Colloquium Prague, Czech Republic, January 2016a. As of August 1, 2018:
https://www.cert.br/docs/palestras/certbr-tcfirst2016.pdf

———, "Lessons Learned from the Rio2016 Summer Olympic Games," presentation at the San José FIRST Technical Colloquium, San José, Costa Rica, September 2016b. As of August 1, 2018:
https://www.cert.br/docs/palestras/certbr-tcfirst2016.pdf

Enomoto, Tsuyoshi, director, Information Science and Technology, Japanese Ministry of Education, Culture, Sports, Science, and Technology, "Cybersecurity Strategy in Japan and Countermeasures for Cyber Threats by MEXT," presentation slides, November 1, 2016. As of August 1, 2018:
https://www.oasis-open.org/events/sites/oasis-open.org.events/files/2.0%20 MEXT%20Tsuyoshi%20Enomoto.pdf

European Network Information Security Agency, "Threat Taxonomy," spreadsheet, September 2016. As of August 1, 2018:
https://www.enisa.europa.eu/topics/threat-risk-management/threats-and-trends/ enisa-threat-landscape/threat-taxonomy/view

Finnegan, Matthew, "Olympics Was Targeted by State-Sponsored Cyber Attack, Says LOCOG CIO," *Computer World UK*, November 20, 2013. As of August 1, 2018:
http://www.computerworlduk.com/it-management/ olympics-was-targeted-by-state-sponsoredcyber-attack-says-locog-cio-3490186

Foer, Franklin, "The Man Who Ruined the World Cup," *Slate*, June 28, 2002. As of September 7, 2018:
http://www.slate.com/articles/sports/sports_nut/2002/06/the_man_who_ruined_ the_world_cup.html

Francescani, Chris, "Brazil Superhackers Stalk Olympic Tourists," NBC News, August 11, 2016. As of August 1, 2018:
http://www.nbcnews.com/storyline/2016-rio-summer-olympics/ brazil-superhackers-stalk-olympic-tourists-n625661

Genik, Lynne, and Luc Beaudoin, Defense Research and Development Canada and Canada Cyber Incident Response Centre, "Cyber Security Information Sharing: A Case Study of Olympic Proportions," presentation at the CRHNet Symposium, Vancouver, Canada, October 24, 2012. As of August 1, 2018:
http://www.crhnet.ca/sites/default/files/library/T1B_genik.pdf

Glick, Bryan, "CIO Interview: Gerry Pennell, CIO, London 2012 Olympics," *Computer Weekly*, October 14, 2011. As of August 1, 2018:
http://www.computerweekly.com/news/2240111814/
CIO-interview-Gerry-Pennell-CIO-London-2012-Olympics

Government of Japan, *Cybersecurity Strategy*, September 4, 2015. As of August 1, 2018:
http://www.nisc.go.jp/eng/pdf/cs-strategy-en.pdf

Government of Japan Cabinet Secretariat, Basic Act on the Formation of an Advanced Information and Telecommunications Network Society, November 29, 2000. As of August 1, 2018:
http://japan.kantei.go.jp/it/it_basiclaw/summary.html

Gross, Jon, and Cylance SPEAR Team, *Operation Dust Storm*, Irvine, Calif.: Cylance, undated. As of August 1, 2018:
https://www.cylance.com/content/dam/cylance/pdfs/reports/Op_Dust_Storm_Report.pdf

Haq, Thoufique, Ned Moran, Sai Vashisht, and Mike Scott, *Operation Quantum Entanglement*, Milpitas, Calif.: FireEye, 2014. As of August 1, 2018:
https://www.fireeye.com/content/dam/fireeye-www/global/en/current-threats/pdfs/wp-operation-quantum-entanglement.pdf

Hathaway, Melissa, Chris Demchak, Jason Kerben, Jennifer McArdle, and Francesca Spidalieri, *Japan: Cyber Readiness at a Glance*, Arlington, Va.: Potomac Institute for Policy Studies, September 2016. As of August 1, 2018:
http://www.potomacinstitute.org/images/CRI/CRI_Japan_Profile_PIPS.pdf

Hoare, Oliver, UK Home Office, "London 2012: Cyber Security," presentation slides, undated. As of August 1, 2018:
https://www.ipa.go.jp/files/000037535.pdf

Information-Technology Promotion Agency, "About IPA/ISEC," webpage, undated. As of August 1, 2018:
https://www.ipa.go.jp/security/english/aboutisec-e.html

International Olympic Committee, "The Winter Olympic Games," factsheet, September 2014. As of August 1, 2018:
https://stillmed.olympic.org/Documents/Reference_documents_Factsheets/The_Olympic_Winter_Games.pdf

———, "The Games of the Olympiad," factsheet, January 2017. As of August 1, 2018:
https://stillmed.olympic.org/media/Document%20Library/OlympicOrg/Factsheets-Reference-Documents/Games/OG/Factsheet-The-Games-of-the-Olympiad-January-2017.pdf

International Organization for Standardization, "ISO 31000:2009, Risk Management," webpage, undated. As of August 1, 2018:
https://www.iso.org/iso-31000-risk-management.html

Ishikawa, Yoshihiro, *Cyber Grid View Technical Report: Attackers That Target Critical Infrastructure Providers in Japan*, Vol. 2, Tokyo, Japan: LAC Co., 2016. As of August 1, 2018:
https://www.lac.co.jp/english/report/pdf/cgview_vol2_en.pdf

ISO—*See* International Organization for Standardization.

Japan Computer Emergency Response Team Coordination Center, "About JPCERT/CC," webpage, undated. As of August 1, 2018:
https://www.jpcert.or.jp/english/pr

Japan Times, "Japan's Weak Cyberdefense," December 26, 2016. As of August 1, 2018:
https://www.japantimes.co.jp/opinion/2016/12/26/commentary/japan-commentary/japans-weak-cyberdefense

———, "Government to Hold Massive Anti-Cyberattack Drill for 2020 Tokyo Olympics," January 5, 2017a. As of August 1, 2018:
https://www.japantimes.co.jp/news/2017/01/05/national/government-hold-massive-anti-cyberattack-drill-2020-tokyo-olympics

———, "With Three Years to Go, Some Worried Japan Unprepared for Olympic Cyberattack," July 21, 2017b.

Japanese Ministry of Foreign Affairs, "Japan's Security Policy," webpage, undated. As of August 1, 2018:
https://www.mofa.go.jp/policy/security/index.html

Japanese National Information Security Policy Council, *The Second National Strategy on Information Security Aiming for Strong "Individual" and "Society" in IT Age*, February 3, 2009. As of August 1, 2018:
http://www.nisc.go.jp/eng/pdf/national_strategy_002_eng.pdf

Jenkins, Brian Michael, RAND Corporation, *Is Al Qaeda's Internet Strategy Working?* testimony before the Counterterrorism and Intelligence Subcommittee, Homeland Security Committee, U.S. House of Representatives, Santa Monica, Calif.: RAND Corporation, CT-371, 2011. As of August 1, 2018:
https://www.rand.org/pubs/testimonies/CT371.html

Jordan, Tim, and Paul A. Taylor, *Hacktivism and Cyberwars: Rebels with a Cause?* New York: Routledge, 2004.

JPCERT/CC—*See* Japan Computer Emergency Response Team Coordination Center.

Kassens-Noor, Eva, and Tatsuya Fukushige, "Olympic Technologies: Tokyo 2020 and Beyond: The Urban Technology Metropolis," *Journal of Urban Technology*, July 1, 2016.

Kimura, Misaki, "2016 in Review: Top Cyber Security Trends in Japan," blog post, JPCERT, January 25, 2017. As of August 1, 2018:
http://blog.jpcert.or.jp/2017/01/2016-in-review-top-cyber-security-trends-in-japan.html

Koebler, Jason, "The Man Who Broke Ticketmaster," *Motherboard*, February 10, 2017. As of August 1, 2018:
https://motherboard.vice.com/en_us/article/mgxqb8/the-man-who-broke-ticketmaster

Magee, Will, "How the 2002 World Cup Became the Most Controversial Tournament in Recent Memory," *Vice Sports*, July 18, 2017. As of September 7, 2018:
https://sports.vice.com/en_uk/article/ywgx4y/how-the-2002-world-cup-became-the-most-controversial-tournament-in-recent-memory

Mandiant, *APT1: Exposing One of China's Cyber Espionage Units*, Alexandria, Va., 2013. As of August 1, 2018:
https://www.fireeye.com/content/dam/fireeye-www/services/pdfs/mandiant-apt1-report.pdf

Manning, Chelsea E., "The Years Since I Was Jailed for Releasing the 'War Diaries' Have Been a Rollercoaster," *The Guardian*, May 27, 2015. As of August 1, 2018:
https://www.theguardian.com/commentisfree/2015/may/27/anniversary-chelsea-manning-arrest-war-diaries

Maza, Cristina, "Cyber Security Training Now Underway in Japan," *Phnom Penh Post*, March 1, 2017. As of August 1, 2018:
http://www.phnompenhpost.com/national/cyber-security-training-now-underway-japan

Meyers, C., S. Powers, and D. Faissol, *Taxonomies of Cyber Adversaries and Attacks: A Survey of Incidents and Approaches*, Livermore, Calif.: Lawrence Livermore National Laboratory, 2009. As of August 1, 2018:
https://e-reports-ext.llnl.gov/pdf/379498.pdf

Miller, J. Berkshire, "How Will Japan's New NSC Work?" *The Diplomat*, January 29, 2014. As of August 1, 2018:
http://thediplomat.com/2014/01/how-will-japans-new-nsc-work

Morris, Chris, "Experts Warn of Hacking Threat at Rio Olympics," CNBC, July 19, 2016. As of August 1, 2018:
https://www.cnbc.com/2016/07/18/experts-warn-of-hacking-threat-at-rio-olympics.html

Murphy, Ian, "Japan Trains Cyber Teams for 2020 Olympics," *Enterprise Times*, February 7, 2017. As of August 1, 2018:
https://www.enterprisetimes.co.uk/2017/02/07/japan-trains-cyber-teams-2020-olympics

Nakashima, Ellen, "The NSA Has Linked the WannaCry Computer Worm to North Korea," *Washington Post*, June 14, 2017.

National Center of Incident Readiness and Strategy for Cybersecurity, *Next Cybersecurity Strategy (Outline)*, 2017.

Nikkei Asian Review, "Japan to Deepen Ranks of Network Defenders with Eye to Olympics," July 16, 2015. As of August 1, 2018:
https://asia.nikkei.com/Politics-Economy/Policy-Politics/
Japan-to-deepen-ranks-of-network-defenders-with-eye-to-Olympics

Otake, Tomoko, "1.25 Million Affected by Japan Pension Service Hack," *Japan Times*, June 1, 2015. As of August 1, 2018:
https://www.japantimes.co.jp/news/2015/06/01/national/crime-legal/
japan-pension-system-hacked-1-25-million-cases-personal-data-leaked

Paganini, Pierluigi, "Operation Dust Storm, Hackers Target Japanese Critical Infrastructure," *Security Affairs*, February 24, 2016. As of August 1, 2018:
http://securityaffairs.co/wordpress/44749/cyber-crime/operation-dust-storm.html

Perez, Evan, "First on CNN: U.S. Investigators Find Proof of Cyberattack on Ukraine Power Grid," CNN, February 3, 2016. As of August 1, 2018:
http://www.cnn.com/2016/02/03/politics/cyberattack-ukraine-power-grid

Perlroth, Nicole, "More Evidence Points to North Korea in Ransomware Attack," *New York Times*, May 22, 2017.

Pitcher, Robert, cyber incident handler, Public Safety Canada, "Vancouver 2010 Olympics Lessons Learned: Cyber," presentation at the FIRST Conference, Vienna, Austria, June 15, 2011. As of August 1, 2018:
https://www.first.org/resources/papers/conference2011/pitcher-robert-slides.pdf

Polityuk, Pavel, and Alessandra Prentice, "Ukraine Says to Review Cyber Defenses After Airport Targeted from Russia," Reuters, January 18, 2016. As of August 1, 2018:
http://www.reuters.com/article/
us-ukraine-cybersecurity-malware-idUSKCN0UW0R0

Ponemon Institute, *Advanced Threats in Retail Companies: A Study of North America and EMEA*, Traverse City, Mich., May 2015. As of August 1, 2018:
http://pages.arbornetworks.com/rs/arbor/images/Ponemon_Advanced%20
Threats%20in%20Retail%20fnl.pdf

Prime Minister of Japan and His Cabinet, "Fundamental Structure of the Government of Japan," webpage, undated(a). As of August 1, 2018:
http://japan.kantei.go.jp/constitution_and_government_of_japan/fundamental_
e.html

———,"IT Strategic Headquarters," webpage, undated(b). As of August 1, 2018:
http://japan.kantei.go.jp/policy/it/index_e.html

Randazzo, Marissa Reddy, Michelle Keeney, Eileen Kowalski, Dawn Cappelli, and Andrew Moore, *Insider Threat Study: Illicit Cyber Activity in the Banking and Finance Sector*, Pittsburgh, Pa.: Software Engineering Institute, Carnegie Mellon University, June 2005. As of August 1, 2018:
https://resources.sei.cmu.edu/asset_files/TechnicalReport/2005_005_001_14420.pdf

Robertson, Jordan, and Michael Riley, "The Map That Shows Why a Pipeline Explosion in Turkey Matters to the U.S.," *Bloomberg*, December 20, 2014. As of August 1, 2018:
https://www.bloomberg.com/news/2014-12-10/the-map-that-shows-why-a-pipeline-explosion-in-turkey-matters-to-the-u-s-.html

Rogers, Marcus K., "A Two-Dimensional Circumplex Approach to the Development of a Hacker Taxonomy," *Digital Investigation*, Vol. 3, No. 2, June 2006, pp. 97–102.

Rogers, Marcus K., Kathryn Seigfried, and Kirti Tidke, "Self-Reported Computer Criminal Behavior: A Psychological Analysis," *Digital Investigation*, Vol. 3, Supplement, September 2006, pp. 116–120.

Seebruck, Ryan, "A Typology of Hackers: Classifying Cyber Malfeasance Using a Weighted Arc Circumplex Model," *Digital Investigation*, Vol. 14, September 2015, pp. 36–45.

Shaw, Eric D., "The Role of Behavioral Research and Profiling in Malicious Cyber Insider Investigations," *Digital Investigation*, Vol. 3, No. 1, March 2006, pp. 20–31.

Sisario, Ben, "Congress Moves to Curb Ticket Scalping, Banning Bots Used Online," *New York Times*, December 8, 2016.

Smith, Kevin B., "Typologies, Taxonomies, and the Benefits of Policy Classification," *Policy Studies Journal*, Vol. 30, No. 3, August 2002, pp. 379–395.

Sousa, Gregory, "Numbers of Participating Countries in Olympic Games Through the Years," *WorldAtlas.com*, last updated April 25, 2017. As of August 1, 2018:
http://www.worldatlas.com/articles/olympic-games-over-the-years-number-of-participating-countries.html

Spaaij, Ramón, "Terrorism and Security at the Olympics: Empirical Trends and Evolving Research Agendas," *International Journal of the History of Sport*, Vol. 33, No. 4, February 2016, pp. 451–468.

Stoneburner, Gary, *Underlying Technical Models for Information Technology Security*, National Institute of Standards and Technology, SP 800-33, December 2001 (withdrawn on August 1, 2018). As of August 1, 2018:
http://csrc.nist.gov/publications/nistpubs/800-33/sp800-33.pdf

Symantec, "Ransom.Wannacry," webpage, undated. As of August 1, 2018:
https://www.symantec.com/security_response/writeup.
jsp?docid=2017-051310-3522-99

Symantec Security Response, "WannaCry: Ransomware Attacks Show Strong Links to Lazarus Group," *Symantec Official Blog*, May 22, 2017. As of August 1, 2018:
https://www.symantec.com/connect/blogs/wannacry-ransomware-attacks-show-strong-links-lazarus-group

Taylor, Tracy, and Kristine Toohey, "Perceptions of Terrorism Threats at the 2004 Olympic Games: Implications for Sport Events," *Journal of Sport and Tourism*, Vol. 12, No. 2, 2007, pp. 99–114.

Toohey, Kristine, and Tracy Taylor, "Mega Events, Fear, and Risk: Terrorism at the Olympic Games," *Journal of Sport Management*, Vol. 22, No. 4, July 2008, pp. 451–469.

Trend Micro, "Japan Pension System Gets Hacked, Exposes 1.25M Records," June 2, 2015. As of August 1, 2018:
https://www.trendmicro.com/vinfo/us/security/news/cyber-attacks/japan-pension-system-hacked-exposes-125m-records

———,"Security Predictions: The Next Tier," December 6, 2016. As of August 1, 2018:
https://www.trendmicro.com/vinfo/us/security/research-and-analysis/predictions/2017

Tsunehira, Furuya, "The Roots and Realities of Japan's Cyber-Nationalism," Sasakawa Peace Foundation USA, January 29, 2016. As of August 1, 2018:
https://spfusa.org/nippon-com/the-roots-and-realities-of-japans-cyber-nationalism

United Nations Office on Drugs and Crime, *United Nations Convention Against Transnational Organized Crime and the Protocols Thereto*, 2004. As of August 1, 2018:
https://www.unodc.org/documents/middleeastandnorthafrica/organised-crime/UNITED_NATIONS_CONVENTION_AGAINST_TRANSNATIONAL_ORGANIZED_CRIME_AND_THE_PROTOCOLS_THERETO.pdf

Urano, Akira, *The Japanese Underground*, Trend Micro, 2015. As of August 1, 2018:
https://www.trendmicro.de/cloud-content/us/pdfs/security-intelligence/white-papers/wp-the-japanese-underground.pdf

US-CERT—*See* U.S. Computer Emergency Readiness Team.

U.S. Computer Emergency Response Team, "Security Tip (ST17-001): Securing the Internet of Things," revised November 17, 2017. As of September 7, 2018:
https://www.us-cert.gov/ncas/tips/ST17-001

———, "Alert (TA17-132A): Indicators Associated with WannaCry Ransomware," revised June 7, 2018. As of August 1, 2018:
https://www.us-cert.gov/ncas/alerts/TA17-132A

Von Behr, Ines, Anais Reding, Charlie Edwards, and Luke Gribbon, *Radicalisation in the Digital Era: The Use of the Internet in 15 Cases of Terrorism and Extremism*, Santa Monica, Calif.: RAND Corporation, RR-453-RE, 2013. As of August 1, 2018:
http://www.rand.org/pubs/research_reports/RR453.html

Yamaguchi, Jiro, "Signs of the Far Right in Japan's Politics," *Japan Times*, August 29, 2017. As of August 1, 2018:
https://www.japantimes.co.jp/opinion/2017/08/29/commentary/japan-commentary/signs-far-right-japans-politics

About the Authors

Cynthia Dion-Schwarz is a senior scientist at the RAND Corporation focusing predominantly on cybersecurity technology and policy. She has broad expertise in information technology and cyber operations. Her other work has explored science and technology, research and development, and planning and acquisition in the defense and intelligence communities.

Nathan Ryan is an analyst at RAND Europe focusing on topics in cybersecurity and technology. His previous research has examined interagency participation in joint military exercises, and he was a member of the Strategy and Statecraft in Cyberspace research team at Australian National University.

Julia A. Thompson is a defense analyst at the RAND Corporation who studies the health of the defense industrial base, crisis management, South Asian security, and nuclear and conventional deterrence. She has co-edited volumes of essays on deterrence stability, antisatellite weapons, and Sino-American space relations.

Erik Silfversten is a senior analyst at RAND Europe focusing on cybersecurity, cyber defense, and emerging technologies. He has worked on several high-profile studies for national governments and international organizations, including the European Defence Agency and NATO. He previously oversaw policy and strategic development at IMPACT, the cybersecurity partner of the International Telecommunication Union.

Giacomo Persi Paoli is a research leader in RAND Europe's Defence, Security, and Infrastructure Group, overseeing its National Security and Resilience research portfolio. His expertise spans topics in defense and security, including counterterrorism, maritime security, border security, risk analysis, arms control and illicit trafficking, and defense market analysis and includes studies for a range of national and international clients.